MAKING A POINT

MAKING A POINT

A BUSINESS OWNER'S FIELD COMPANION

JOANNE CAMPAGNA

White Falcon Publishing

Making A Point
Joanne Campagna

Published by White Falcon Publishing
Chandigarh, India

First Edition, 2025

Cover design by Nicholas Switalski, 2025
Cover image by Joanne Campagna

The contents of this book have been certified and timestamped on the Gnosis blockchain as a permanent proof of existence. Scan the QR code or visit the URL given on the back cover to verify the blockchain certification for this book.

Paperback ISBN: 978-93-49311-42-8
Hardback ISBN: 979-8-89222-563-2

Dedication

Dedicated to Finley Sebastien Biscay's Black Pearl, the first Ontario-born Barbet, the first Barbet to title in nearly every available dock jumping venue in the U.S. and Canada, the author's first "heart dog," and the inspiration for her first small business, Canine Splash, LLC. Thus began the intersection of her professional passion and her personal love.

Introduction

It is said that you only live once. Well, then, blending the passions of your life is a must.

I have always loved animals. So, the fact that I became involved in a community centered around a rare breed of dog should not come as a surprise. The trajectory of my personal life and, eventually, my professional life took a very different path due to my involvement and passion for the Barbet (more commonly known as the French water dog).

I spent the majority of my full-time working years as a banker in small business, business banking, and commercial banking. During that time, I was privileged to work with many diverse business owners, both based in Buffalo, New York, and our "border" city, Toronto, Canada (it's about an hour and a half from my hometown). Both my personal and professional lives crossed the border for as long as I can remember. It inspired me to create a new business concept, at the time, of indoor dog swimming. I had recently brought into my home a Barbet, a breed that was just developing in North America. Business and Barbet became my passions, and whenever I could weave them together was an ideal day!

My professional career included many leadership programs and exposed me to businesses of all sizes—with all types of financial needs. I sat on the boards of prestigious institutions, including the local Small Business Administration Advisory Council, for years. These volunteer efforts expanded my knowledge of the business field and helped me direct my career along an ever-expanding track of business-related topics.

When I took early retirement from my corporate profession in late 2019, just before the COVID pandemic, I started my own business consulting practice. I wanted to contribute something on a routine basis connected to my enjoyment of business consulting, so I also created a weekly blog. I made sure to include all aspects of being a business owner that I had become familiar with, both as a small business owner and as an advisor to others. For my blog, I wanted the "read" to be quick, acknowledging the busy schedules of business owners; I also aimed to make it humorous and informative.

Using my eldest Pied (black & white) Barbet, The Marquis de Lafayette, aka Lâffey, as inspiration, I named it "Making A Point." As a gun dog or sporting dog, the Barbet will point at, flush, and retrieve prey. The dog's point is a singular focus on the target and seemed a great metaphor to discuss business topics as well. So, I carried the theme of a working field dog or "gun dog" into the weekly business blog entries.

In addition to my decades of commercial banking expertise, I also had firsthand experience in executive peer advisory groups (EPAGs), both as a member myself and by hearing from clients over the years who also belonged to such networks. This inspired me to start my own EPAG, focused on professional women. Because membership in these groups is often based solely on revenue size, most professionals who are solopreneurs don't qualify. I called it IWON, Illuminate Women Owners Network. I often write my articles based on themes or topics raised by this group. And since everyone in the group is also a pet owner, it carries my theme of business and pets forward.

One of my first pets was a terrier. He had a lot of fear issues, so after a few years, I consulted an animal behavioralist. I came to realize that my pet's life would improve if he had a strong leader companion. So, I began my quest for a second dog, one that could forge a tight bond with me and my terrier. I had been reading about the Barbet for over a decade. It was a breed that was in the European gun dog group, similar to the sporting group here in the U.S. Like many European dog breeds, World War II had reduced its ranks to near extinction. Many of the attributes I had read describing the Barbet were those I felt would be ideal for my household. But how to find one?

Some say it was fate, others just luck, but I came across a website in Ontario, Canada, just over the border. It was a Canadian Barbet breeder who was anticipating the first-born litter of Barbet in Ontario. I emailed her, and the following weekend, I found myself dragging my close friend across the border. Little did I know my life was about to be completely changed.

We met the breeder at an outdoor Canadian Kennel Club dog show. The weather was stormy, with strong winds, torrential rain, thunder, and lightning. But, as the saying goes, "the show must go on." Her friend was caring for some of the available puppies while she showed the adult dogs. Among that group of puppies was the one I would eventually bring home. At the time, his name was Sebastien, but he became known as Finley. Finley captured my heart and changed how I not only lived my life but also the direction it went.

Finley became my first "heart dog." If you are not a dog person, this means that we formed a special canine-human bond. He was my true companion; his zest for activity and water led me to my first business venture, Canine Splash. Another friend with a passion for dogs and I went in together, investing the money we had each inherited from family, and created an indoor dog swimming center. We patterned it after the pools used in the dog sport of dock diving. This part-time business venture allowed me to truly walk in the shoes of the business owners I had worked with for decades. What a revelation!

In a three-year timeframe, just a few of the lessons I learned and the experiences I had included:

- How challenging it can be to have a business partner.
- How to manage "dog parents" who were screaming and jumping up and down, saying, "I just want my dog to swim," when their dog's height was taller than the water was deep.
- Identified that our triple net lease was the worst type for a start-up part-time business.
- Researched the acceptance of credit cards while managing the risk of carrying cash on hand.

- (This is true!) I received a call while I was in New York City to hear our team frantically reporting that there was a bat dive-bombing the dogs in the pool.

Yes, this is what it can be like to own a small business at times: "bats gone crazy," literally!

On the plus side, I made close friends on both sides of the border; we had many Canadian dog owners driving down to swim their dogs. I learned about the science behind humidity and indoor pools—hint: cover the pool when not in use. I was interviewed on television about our concept and received inquiries about franchising, all while having a great time seeing how much my clients (the dogs) loved the pools. They never wanted to leave.

We had a great experience bringing in interns from the local college's animal behavior program. It was a wonderful way to help the students understand what the exercise of swimming meant to both dogs and their owners. The interns helped us keep the lights on for the duration of the lease while earning required field internships for their degree. The appropriate use of interns can truly add value for all involved.

We created a new concept for dog exercise, made a splash in the local community, seemed to deal with every possible aspect of business ownership, and then closed the business at the end of the lease. We sold one of our pools and decking to my friend who owns the local dog daycare center we still attend. So, Finley's pool and legacy live on in the lives of many dogs who have been able to swim at daycare for more than ten years now.

Creating, opening a business, selling assets, and closing a business, all in a short timeframe of a few years. So many of my experiences here manifest in the book chapters. From understanding commercial leases to how to legally manage "bats in the belfry", to how to handle disgruntled customers or clients, to amassing the best circle of trusted advisors, all of these are topics in the book. You really cannot make up these experiences—they are credible because they really happened!

One of the hardest lessons I learned as a business owner was to never design a logo or start a business for a specific pet in your life. Sadly, their lives are, for the most part, so much shorter than most of ours. Two years after closing Canine Splash, my beloved Finley became sick and died within a week; he was only eight years old. A necropsy showed he had brain cancer in the frontal lobe. It was devastating.

It struck me at the time that if Canine Splash had still been open, I was not sure if I would have been able to carry on. So, as I looked through the rearview mirror of my life, closing the business had been the right decision. I had never even considered this possibility when I started the business. Now, it is foremost on my mind for anything I create.

At the time that I lost Finley, my other dog, The Marquis de Lafayette, aka Lâffey, was just over a year old. Without him and my older dog, Kolby, moving past the loss of Finley would have been unimaginable. I decided then that I always needed to have at least a few dogs at any given time.

Another realization after Finley died was how awful it was to have had a dog with a very popular name. When my backyard neighbors brought home their own Finn, I became determined to use more obscure names. With my interest in history and the American Revolutionary War, I identified French nobility who helped win the war against the British. This naming process has served us well so far and hopefully will into the future.

I was one of the founding four Barbet owners of The Barbet Fanciers Club of America, the forerunner to the American Kennel Club parent club, The Barbet Club of America. I learned all about starting up 501(c)(7) not-for-profit clubs. I was the treasurer and then vice president. It was like starting another business in many ways, all part of my Business & Barbet experience!

I have not been involved in the club for years now; as a pet owner, my time had been completed there. (Breeders stepped up and took over the club.)

Looking for other ways to pair my passion for this rare breed with my career interests, I started writing weekly blogs featuring Lâffey and friends, in which I addressed many of the aspects of being a business owner that I listed above. Additionally, talking to other business owners as part of my professional career allowed me to augment my own experiences. While we might have different-sized and shaped feet, shoes, or paws, we were all walking the same walk.

Shortly before starting the adventure of compiling my online blog articles into book form, a Canadian Barbet friend told me how her daughter, studying in business school, began reading my weekly blogs and sharing them with her classmates. They found them entertaining and educational... and a quick read. My writing provided insight into the day of a business owner that none of them could experience firsthand yet. If any of them decide to become a business advisor, such as an accountant or lawyer, they would have a bird's-eye view of some of the things their future clients might go through.

At the same time, a friend told me how her colleague was using a few of my articles in executive management training. The lightbulb went off, and I thought perhaps the combination of my Canine Splash experiences, my professional career, and my current solopreneur consulting practice would work well as a book and bring knowledge and humor to more households. And, of course, keeping the dog theme would be paramount in any literary endeavor.

And here I am, almost two decades later. I call many of my Barbet friends my closest friends. I successfully parlayed the combo platter of my post-banking career with my interest in dogs, particularly the Barbet, into operating my own business consulting firm with a focus on peer advisory for other women executives and sharing my experiences with others through my blog. My worlds have collided in the best way. When my passion became my livelihood, I became a stronger, happier person. And my life has truly "gone to the dogs."

So, join me in the field of business and enjoy references to the canine world that express the many topics business owners encounter. Have a laugh, learn a bit, and use this as a guide for quick reference to a specific topic. Most of all, enjoy the experience—my hope is that readers may learn to be better business owners, business students, or simply acknowledge the benefits of a laugh or a smile as they go through their daily business life.

Vive Le Propriétaire d'entreprise!

Joanne Campagna

Contents

Section I

Natural Instinct

Business Owner Characteristics

Instinct can be applied to just about any species. It is fascinating to watch a dog from the traditional working or herding groups, one without formal training, engage in behavior for which it is bred. If you have a dog that "instinctively" knows how to point or flush out birds, you will know what I am referring to. The next time you see a pet owner trying to keep their dog from chasing a squirrel up a tree, think "instinct."

For those dogs without a natural talent, consider the importance of training. Many, but not all, can be trained to excel at certain sports. They may not lead the pack in awards, but you can see the fun and excitement they experience in their behavior throughout the journey.

In the business world, it's no different. Some people just have a natural talent or instinct for entrepreneurial tendencies, while for others, technical expertise and training can help launch them on the road to success.

In Section I, readers will find business commentary addressing what it takes to be a small business owner or a solopreneur. Not everyone wants to be on their own and responsible for leading. Before you act, read up on the importance of being yourself!

- Chapter 1: On the Hunt
- Chapter 2: Different Ways to Be a Leader

- Chapter 3: The Passion Play
- Chapter 4: Your Mirror Image
- Chapter 5: Getting Paid: Know Your Value
- Chapter 6: The Importance of Being Me
- Chapter 7: Executive Leadership

Chapter 1

On the Hunt

Building your own business, particularly if you have never done this before, can feel like you are surrounded by a proverbial open field—do not let it overwhelm you. Take control of your idea, and with the proper field support along the way, you can overcome any obstacles you might face.

Illuminate Business Consulting, LLC is the second such entity I have created. Years ago, I created a new concept with a friend and business partner that involved indoor pools for recreational dog swimming. While I was able to use some of the lessons learned from that experience, back then, I had a business partner to split all the tasks with. This time, it was just me. While I am always up for a challenge, I forgot how much a new business owner has to contend with—sometimes I felt like I was in a circus and my job was to juggle all the balls, hoping that none fell! (But, surely, if they did, my ball-obsessed dog would have been there to grab them and toss them back at me for an endless game of fetch!)

Here are some of the concepts a new business owner needs to grapple with:

- What will your business be named? Is the name available for incorporation in the state you are in, and is it free of trademarks?
- What types of insurance will you need?
- Where will you locate your business? Make sure you understand terms such as triple net leases, CAM, personal recourse, or guaranty.
- Do you have the appropriate advisors, i.e., an attorney, accountant, realtor, etc., to guide you?

- What office furniture or equipment do you need? Be prepared to spend days, not hours, on this task. Unless you have hired a facilities coordinator or architect to design your space, it will all fall on you. Color, price point, how many drawers, how many cabinets, what color paint in the office, window treatments, etc.
- What about benefits and, most importantly, health insurance? This can be the subject of a full-year MBA project!

These are but a few of the many administrative tasks a new business owner must embrace, understand, and execute when on the hunt for their perfect business. You can go it alone as I did, but I have the benefit of having done this before and of having spent over twenty years assisting entrepreneurs in achieving their goals and dreams. You can reach out to the U.S. Small Business Administration's Small Business Development Center (SBDC) in your area, or you can seek the assistance of a business advisor, such as your accountant, to help guide you on your path.

For start-ups where you have no experience, the SBDC is truly your best path. They can assist you with writing a business plan and provide counseling on your new venture. Their services are usually complimentary. If you are an experienced professional seeking to start your own practice after working for someone else for years, reach out to a business advisor. They can likely fast-track all of this while you minimize the time between your current position and your ownership position, lessening the timeframe you are away from clients, patients, or customers.

Dogs may often look to their handlers for cues for the next step in the field and seek direction and reinforcement to complete their tasks. Like their canine companions, business owners should consider following the advice of their handlers, the SBDC, or their chosen business advisor. Research your options, read through this book, and consider the support you are most comfortable with for your company. If you bring a dog into your home, you likely will have preferences for size, temperament, and coat; define your preferences for your business companions in the same detail. With the proper synergy, you can complete your achievements sooner rather than later.

Chapter 2

Different Ways to Be a Business Leader

Business leaders and owners come in many different profiles. The good news is that there is not only one style that can be successful.

There is one very familiar type: the extroverted, charismatic person. They walk into any room and immediately draw attention. I call them "the politicians." They often have something that compels others to follow them. It may be ideology; it may be their look, their sound, or their message. They have the ability to move among varied types of situations with style and sometimes grace. They always seem to remember you. They have that presence about them, which can sometimes captivate onlookers. They can be funny, a bit on the loud side, and usually quite charming.

But the good news is that there are many other types of people who are quite successful as business leaders or owners. One does not need to be a "natural politician" to achieve success. In the decades I have been around business leaders and owners, I have observed how different each one is. Another profile I've identified is "the technician." They are usually on the quiet side, perhaps what many would call cerebral. You can practically see them internally assessing their next word or action. They are very logical, great at organization, and can always provide insight in their chosen field. They tend to be more introverted than extroverted, rejecting any pomp or circumstance around their leadership. Their expertise can be the fuel that propels their business and can certainly be their competitive advantage.

So, if you have technical knowledge but don't happen to be the "room-pleaser," no worries; you can be just as successful!

My eldest Barbet dog is a politician. He draws attention everywhere he goes, loves to kiss anyone who will let him, and he really loves the ladies, both human and canine! He lights up any event in which he participates. He is always noticed. My other animals and I often find ourselves basking in his glow; we just know we cannot compete with him.

So, take comfort in knowing that to be successful in business, you just need to be yourself. Play up those attributes that make you knowledgeable in your field, sought after in your industry, and an expert whom others want to emulate. If you do all that, you will have a platform from which you can excel.

Chapter 3

The Passion Play

One characteristic successful businesspeople share is their passion. Similar to dogs—who have a strong desire to compete and succeed in anything from fetch to hunting—people's passion for rewards and results is what compels them onward.

It has been observed that I am very resilient. Someone once said it was like I fell overboard off a ship and just kept climbing back on board. (The person who made this analogy became a professional mentor in my career.) I think about their comment whenever I must start over, try a different approach, or take an unfamiliar path. It is that desire, or passion, to succeed or make something better that motivates me. And I'll bet that without it, you would not likely be reading this book!

I am fascinated by the vastly different places from which business owners and leaders draw their inspiration. It comes in many varieties. Some had it instilled while growing up, perhaps from a family business or a driven relative. Some wanted to be as different as possible from their parents—even needing to prove a point. Many, however, seem to be driven by a desire for improvement in their field. Perhaps they have identified a better product or a more unique service and want the opportunity to share it.

Professional services people often find a niche and can promote it by meshing it with their business. Sustainability, climate change, and the environment are great, more recent examples. A focus on a concept like one of these allows architects, engineers, or lawyers to center their practice on the greater good. So, with passion can come the desire to effect change for the greater good, and that can help drive a person to open a business and run it successfully, regardless of their style.

If you have passion, you will know it. If you don't, think a bit harder. There may be something that truly inspires you. Capture that inspiration, turn it into desire or passion, and you will likely have the foundation of a successful journey in opening a new business.

My very driven dog is not equally inspired by all toys. If it squeaks and bounces, he is on it. If it is fluffy or silent, it is likely that it will not elicit his passion for play. People's career paths are no different. Find what inspires you, find what motivates you, and go after it. Passion for your business is an integral aspect of potential success as a business owner or leader.

Chapter 4

Your Mirror Image

The choice to open or expand your own business will likely be one of the most defining decisions in your professional livelihood. As you embark on this journey, it is important to ask yourself what you see in the mirror. Do you see determination, perseverance, and creativity? You will need all these attributes, in addition to your passion, to make your business the success you believe it can be.

Determination is critical. Without the underlying motivation to make your journey successful, it may be challenging to overcome the obstacles that will come your way. Set yourself up for success by believing in yourself, your vision, and your product or service.

My previous business partner and I created our indoor dog swimming business because our dogs loved to swim. They went crazy for water, anywhere they could find it. They were so much fun to watch, so ignited by the prospect of swimming as they entered the building that one could not help but feel the passion and embrace it. In fact, we often used our own dogs' love of the pools to try to encourage new dogs who weren't quite sure about swimming inside an above-ground pool. It worked about 75% of the time. There are just some dogs that will never swim and some that just won't swim inside with the different sounds and smells. Without their enthusiasm for all things water, likely our business would never have been created. We even had people who just wanted to come and watch our dogs jump, swim, and retrieve. It was mesmerizing and uplifting—an experience likely not easily forgotten.

Like our past dogs above, people can feel that innate drive as you start to pitch your new business. Not all of us are talented salespeople, but the power of believing that your new business can and will make a difference in someone's life goes a long way. Ultimately, we are all selling something, and it starts with yourself.

Perseverance is another cornerstone of your pathway to success. Enter your new quest with the understanding that you will have to scale obstacles and find solutions outside the box. You are not alone, and that is important to remember. Try to find administrative, financial, and marketing support by relying on those around you—those who may have inspired and encouraged your new journey.

Creativity takes many forms in your new venture. The very fact that you are drawn to forming or expanding a business shows creativity. Look to your advisors for assistance with getting creative—from defining your brand to the formation of services or products. Never stop creating; it will keep your brand fresh and help differentiate you from the competition.

The person in the mirror now is someone you should visit periodically during the life cycle of your business. Reflection is yet another critical component of this process; think about where you are, where you had hoped to be, and where you will take yourself and your business. Once you start on this path, fueled by your determination, perseverance, and creativity, your journey can be a long and fulfilling one.

Hopefully, you will feel that same energy our dogs used to exhibit when bursting through the door and up the stairs to the pool deck. The splash of water once they made it into the pool was always met with collective excitement, as we knew how happy they were and how much they were enjoying the experience. We wanted to jump in with them!

Chapter 5

Getting Paid: Know Your Value

Like it or not, all the passion, desire, or expertise will take you nowhere without being paid for it.

Each of us needs a steady income to cover essentials as well as the extras we choose for ourselves. For me, that would be my dogs and the many activities they require for an enriching life, such as training, daycare, grooming, and titled sports. None of these are free. Throw in children, healthcare, aging parents, and the costs add up. Clearly, money is a factor in what work you choose. And, if you are a business owner, you need to evaluate which jobs or projects you take on and which you don't. Weighing the job, the customer, and the client against the profitability will help you decide.

Our personal value is a result of the personal "brand" we have built. Knowing your value and proudly proclaiming it in the proposals you submit is essential to propelling your business forward. If a potential client expects your services to be free, tries to tell you that you are charging too much, or suggests that they can refer other clients to you in lieu of payment, move on. While there may come a time when pro bono, philanthropic, or community work is right for you, at this stage, you are building a business. You do not need the opportunity to work for free; that does not buy groceries or pay your bills.

I was recently asked to provide a letter of reference for one of my business advisors. It took me ten minutes to write and email it. I value the work that the business advisor did, and I was happy to write a reference. Offering to help someone who has performed good work for you is a natural courtesy that occurs in the course of doing business with others. I did not expect anything in return for writing the reference, and certainly not their services for free in thc future. As a result of this mutually satisfactory business relationship, this advisor is always quick to respond to any of my inquiries or additional work. So, I will invoke another golden rule: Treat others as you would like them to treat you.

I have yet to meet anyone who does not expect to be paid for jobs where their intellectual property, experience, and licensing, if applicable, are required. Intimating that you expect someone's services to be free could insult them to the point that you jeopardize your personal brand's reputation. You never want to be known as the individual, practice, or corporation that does not pay. Your customers or clients may then be few and far between.

Defining your value is research you should do ahead of time. Research your competitors, search online for expected fees, and attend trade seminars. While you might be tempted to discount your services to win a hard-to-get client or break into a new market, charging less should not be a strategy for conducting all your business; rather, it should be a seldomly used tool to expand your business.

There was a time when professional service providers' time could be tax deductible if performing them on a pro-bono or free basis. However, now the IRS guidelines state: "Although you cannot deduct the value of your time or services, you can deduct the expenses you incur while donating your services to a qualified organization." ... Your professional time is not tax deductible." And that professional time is your worth, your personal brand's value. Giving your work away can devalue your business and is not a sustainable model if you are aiming for a successful run.

As you work through your annual business plan, remember to promote your personal value and stay true to yourself. If you do not believe your service or product is worth the asking price, no one else will. Steer clear of those with a handout or wanting "to pick your brain" or asking for a "favor" all the time. They clearly do not value your personal worth, and your time can likely be better spent with those who do.

Chapter 6

The Importance of Being Me

My company, Illuminate, was granted its first WBE Certification a year after I began the venture. This provided me with a national certification as a Women Owned Business Enterprise. Achieving this certification was one of my goals when I decided to start my own consulting business and it highlighted the importance of being *me*.

There are many different types of disadvantaged group certifications available to companies, which are covered later in the book. While not everyone qualifies for one, the idea of certifying a business because its owner is a woman, a veteran, or from an economically disadvantaged district, points to the truth that we are all different, and in those differences can lie our strengths. We each need to highlight those elements of ourselves and our business that emphasize the importance of your individuality, the person behind the title "business owner."

My early career after graduate school often saw me as the only woman in the room or at the table. What was then a somewhat daunting difference for me has now become a beacon of possibility. Playing up this difference now has its advantages when working with governmental or quasi-governmental organizations that need to conduct business with women owned firms from a diversity perspective. Not sure I saw that one coming long ago!

As you identify areas of differentiation for yourself as a business owner, one option to assist you may be the use of personality tests. They can point you in the direction of your strengths and help you understand your weaknesses so you can adequately assess them. The one I took early on in my banking career was the Myers-Briggs Type

Indicator. Its result still rings true for my style and ability to address and cope with challenges, situations, and other personality types. There are many others available; a few of the more well-known include DISC and StrengthsFinder. Do yourself and your career a favor and research the various options and see if there is one or more which can help you navigate your business as its leader.

Being true to yourself is an important approach to running your business. But you can always learn more, both about yourself, and your leadership style. If you do not qualify for a disadvantaged certification or your business would not benefit from one you can qualify for, there are many other ways to differentiate yourself to appeal to new clients.

I continue to ensure that my brand reflects my passion, whether in the causes I sponsor, the colors used in my branding, or my selection of promotional items, such as pens, calendars, tumblers, or blankets. We each bring unique qualities to our positions—identify them, capitalize on them, and use them to tell your story. Never underestimate the importance of being YOU!

Chapter 7

Executive Leadership

One of my first clients in Illuminate asked an interesting and very important question: "How do I become a better leader?"

Consider the application of this question in the sporting dog world. Natural leaders emerge in the canine world, just as in our human world. They are the first to the toy, the ball, to jump in a pool or out of the car; wherever they are motivated, they are leading the pack! Their answer to being a better leader is to run faster, be more focused, and look to their handler for cues. Their passion for their sport of choice will motivate them to lead and leave those behind who are not able to keep up, including their handler or owner!

As you consider your options for becoming a better leader, the good news is that there are reputable organizations available to help you find the answers. I am familiar with many of them because of networking, owning a small business, and leadership roles in commercial banking. Some are free, while others have fees, dues, or tuition. Remember, when you are at this stage, this is an investment in you, your skills, and your future as a better leader.

Early on in my banking career, I was introduced to an Executive Peer Advisory Group (EPAG). Many of my clients were participants in this type of executive coaching for CEOs and business owners. My clients told me how having a peer executive support group enriched their leadership capabilities, allowing them to consider options for their businesses that they could not have realized on their own. EPAGs are offered in most major cities. Membership benefits may include monthly group meetings and monthly one-on-ones with a facilitator or coach, as well as ongoing access to your peers and group leaders for times when you need more immediate advice or attention.

Other executive support and training groups may be at your local chamber of commerce or through individual executive coaches. As a member of a chamber's Executive Exchange Program, I participated in monthly group meetings, which were very helpful. In general, to join a chamber peer group, your organization (or employer, if you are an executive at a company) must be a paying member. My advice to you, as well as to my clients over the years, is that you and your leadership skills are worth the investment, so try not to let the cost dissuade you. Certainly, our dogs have no concept of money, so apply a bit of their "money is no object" mentality here for yourself!

Like any dog or human sport, there are rules governing who can participate in each group: one that is steadfast in any leadership peer exchange group is that no two leaders can come from the same industry. This will allow each person to speak freely, with one of the goals being to garner some competitive tips from members who are not your client, customer, vendor, or competitor. Feel free to ask what other industries will be represented so you can better understand the platform that will be your peer group.

There are other organizations at the city or regional level designed to educate young professionals on its history. An internet search of the name of your city along with the term leadership should yield results for these types of programs. They normally offer leadership experiences that include both classroom teaching and field experiences during a limited time period. When you participate, you are part of the "class" of that year. Class sizes are usually larger than the Peer Support Groups; they can range from 20 to 30 people. Note that these programs are popular, and the application process is competitive. You may need to apply multiple times before being accepted. Again, there may be a significant cost to entry.

My personal experience in leadership programs included Leadership Buffalo, where I visited a high-security prison just outside our city, participated in a ride-along wearing a bulletproof vest with a police officer, and attended the FBI Citizens Academy, where I learned how to shoot multiple guns at a "live" (real bullets used) range. These experiences gave me a better understanding of the entire community and, in these examples, specifically how to keep the community safe as a leader, one of the tenets of community leadership. It was a leadership experience like no other and, sadly, rather relevant today.

The last option for leadership enrichment that I will mention is programs offered through specific sites, usually associated with a college or university, like centers for entrepreneurial leadership. Also, specific to women, your local SBA Women's Business Center may offer Peer Executive Groups to its members. These centers often charge tuition or a membership fee to participate in their programs. Some may even offer a graduate certification. So, there are many options under this classification, and again, the best way to identify these is either to search locally for leadership programs or to ask any of those in your network if they have any recommendations based on their own experience.

Being a leader is a life of its own. You need to enhance it, enrich it, and exercise it, just like you would if you had a dog or any pet. Leadership takes commitment and a willingness to be continuously learning.

As I've discussed, there are many options, and hopefully, one of them will work for you and your leadership budget. And remember, this is an investment in your future, your leadership attributes, and your business. Improving your image, skills, and brand should be your goal.

Step up above the others and join your peers in leadership enrichment. It could change your entire approach to leading your business.

Section I: Points to Ponder

- Business owners and leaders come in many styles; find yours and use it as your platform for success.
- Finding your passion for a product or service will be the foundation of your business.
- Make sure you focus on getting paid and paying any consultants you may be using. Among the many hats small business owners wear is collections. Do not leave anything out in the field; you earned it, collect it.
- Consider joining an Executive Peer Advisory Group, which can provide support and enrichment to your leadership as a business owner.
- Love your business as much as my dog loves his toys!

Section II

Your Pack

Building a Successful Network

Assembling a community is important in nearly every venture we undertake. It also has a place in the dog world, often referred to as "the pack." We cannot do everything alone and require the advice, counsel, leadership, and support of a range of "characters." It takes a community for a business to thrive.

In this section, you will be provided with business commentary regarding advisors, trade associations, organizations, and professionals that should be considered for inclusion in your "pack."

Chapter 8

Who's Your Pack

We have all likely seen or heard of movies that address being popular. They tell a familiar story of who gets to be popular, and who doesn't. Don't most of us want to be part of the "in group"? And, if not, what group are we a part of and why? Or perhaps how do we become more popular?

Many dogs search for their pack. Humans also want to be part of a group. Normally, we gravitate towards those with a common ideology or interests. We search for that pack to belong to in both our personal and professional lives. When it comes to our work, the need to be supported by relevant business owners experiencing similar trials and tribulations that we confront is real. So, how do we fulfill this need?

Trade groups are common in nearly every industry. They provide economic and financial information on your industry, common trends, best and worst practices, and, most importantly, a forum to discuss issues that are important to you. They come in various forms—most licensed professionals have a trade group or association that oversees their licensing in conjunction with the state education department that approves their licensing.

Examples include the American Medical Association, American Veterinary Medical Association, American Dental Association, American Institute of Architects, American Institute of Certified Public Accountants, etc. These professional associations are essential in providing introductions, networking opportunities, and news and updates on the issues or laws impacting the specific field. If you are a professional, it is strongly recommended that you join your specific trade group. It is the foundation and core of your profession. Find the budget to pay the dues, somewhere, somehow. Not belonging can be a severe competitive disadvantage.

So, what about those of us who are not licensed professionals? Where do we find our pack? The first option is a local chamber of commerce. These are wells of information, and beyond being a resource to connect with other businesspeople, they also often offer more competitive health plans, life insurance, and various discounts than a business can find on its own. Their health insurance plans are a great benefit to both the sole proprietor and the small business with employees. They have the infrastructure and the volume of members that can help lower costs. Do not underestimate the value of local chambers. You don't have to participate in all they offer, but you will surely find something that benefits your firm.

Most will also offer young professional clubs or peer support groups along with networking events. I recently attended a Google training sponsored by my local chamber of commerce. The information I gleaned was invaluable. I wouldn't have known about the event itself or the information contained within (how to increase the efficiency of my Google Ads) without my chamber.

Other venues that can help make you feel a part of a greater community include your local SBA centers, area private networking groups, local business or country clubs, or perhaps national peer support organizations. Several of these require an investment upfront, some significant. Do not just join the most expensive affiliation you can find; join the right one for you and your firm. Ask colleagues, ask your influencers—you may be surprised by their suggestions. And they may not require you to write a hefty check.

If you can participate in a leadership program or use a center for entrepreneurs as a resource, you will gain the ability to network and the chance to make lifelong friends.

Take some time to decide which venue and approach are right for you and which one will achieve your personal and professional goals.

Most of us share the desire to belong to a greater cause, and often, finding the pack you run best with goes a long way in getting us down that path and enriching our friendships, our businesses, and, ultimately, our lives.

Chapter 9

Your Professional Business Advisor Circle of Trust

While meeting with a client recently, it became apparent that identifying the business advisors necessary to make their business succeed was a worthwhile exercise. We all need our "circle of trust." Whether it's the actor who made this term iconic (Robert De Niro in *Meet the Parents*) or the business owner struggling to identify the contact information for their various advisors, identifying a circle of trust who will support you is a critical stage in any path forward, whether it be in a high-end RV with Jinxy the cat, or new commercial space for your business.

Many individuals will float in and out of your circle of trust, depending on the current life stage of your business. But there will always be essentials within that circle whose expertise is critical. This group most likely includes your accountant, your attorney, and your banker. They are your first line of defense in organizing your financials, protecting you legally, and providing critical cash and credit management tools for your financial well-being.

Choose wisely to form this group—the people should both understand your goals and share common philosophies and life experiences, along with expertise in your industry. Every business, whether a sole proprietor or a large manufacturer, needs this trio—no exceptions. You should have contact with them, at a minimum, quarterly.

While not in the trio above, your information technology consultant, or IT advisor, is essential to keeping your business humming. In today's digital and electronic age, access to information is absolutely critical for your efficiency and productivity. While less visible than others in your circle, a trusted and communicative IT consultant can be the difference between a good day at the office and a bad one. Find someone you can rely on and respect. They will be a partner in protecting all your intellectual property.

The floaters among your circle of trust may consist of any combination of the following:

Insurance agent – This advisor's level within the circle can vary depending on the nature of your business. Some may consider them essential, while others may only need them annually. If your business has employees, trucks, or cars, or is in a high-risk industry, such as one with exposure to environmental hazards, this advisor will likely be on permanent speed dial.

Graphic designer – With a professional graphic designer in the fold, your business can look polished, professional, and welcoming. Without one, a business's appearance can flounder. Designers help establish your brand, providing the artistic and visual reinforcement of your company and its products or services. The logo and visual elements, such as your website, stationery, and marketing materials, should reflect the image of your company that you have worked hard to establish and are key to how clients perceive you. Do not underestimate the value of a good graphic designer.

Realtor – You hear it often: location, location, location. Finding a respected realtor who understands the marketplace and can identify and negotiate the right space for you defines the physical borders of your business. Placement can be key to gaining a competitive advantage. Asking friends and colleagues for references is a great place to start when identifying and choosing this advisor.

Architect – Whether you are creating the first plans for your office space or preparing for an expansion, a working relationship with an architect whom you trust and who understands your industry can minimize time and pain. While you may not need them as frequently as others in your circle, their input and expertise in helping to define and create your physical space could make or break the outcome of your project. As with others, ask around and do your research to ensure you have the appropriate synergy with this advisor.

Industrial development agency officer – Regardless of the size of your business, you should always consult with your local IDA officer. There may be incentives available for various aspects of your business, and it is certainly worth a conversation. IDA officers are generally in their positions for the long term, so they can get to know you, and you them. Take the time; they can be enormously helpful. They are normally at the county level, so search your county directory for their department.

Business consultant, leadership coach, mentors – At various stages in both your business and personal growth, you may require the services of a strategist. Strategic advisors come in many forms—mentors, leadership or personal coaches, and business consultants. Having individuals from these categories should help provide that different perspective or expertise you might be missing.

Human Resources/Payroll Provider – If your business grows beyond yourself and you do not use consultants to whom you would send a 1099 form of income at year-end, consider adding an HR Professional or Payroll Provider to this list. Often, payroll companies will have a department that can advise on hiring, firing, organizational behavior, and benefits for your staff. As you grow with the addition of employees, this professional advisor will become critical to your daily operations.

As you consider your circle, you may find others whose expertise and support your business may benefit from at times. The key should always be to find that advisor with whom you have mutual respect and a common philosophy. They will help build your foundation and ensure that your circle provides you with the support and information you need.

Chapter 10

Microbusinesses Maximized With Partnering

For many of us who are considered small businesses, we may be what is termed a "microbusiness," also called a micro-enterprise. Instead of hiring and staffing internally, developing working relationships with a few partner affiliations may be a more effective way to grow our businesses.

So, what is a microbusiness?

The Small Business Administration simply states it's a small business employing nine people or fewer. Microbusinesses generally have lower start-up costs and revenue. While the category is loosely defined, many sources indicate that annual revenue is less than $250,000.

As the number of entrepreneurs and self-employed sole proprietors grows, so shall this category. It is a subset of a small business but deserves to be acknowledged and treated differently from the category that can have up to 500 employees. There is a stark difference between firms that are sole proprietors and those with 500 employees.

As a microbusiness, some of the most successful relationships I have seen are what I refer to as contractual partner alliances. From one microbusiness to another, it is a way to outsource work that you, as a sole proprietor, cannot complete on your own. Some examples include human resources, office administration, office receptionist, and (the most intriguing to me) professional service to professional service.

For example, I have seen architects align with other architects, interior designers, or engineers. When a specialty is called for on a project, you will often see a design architect contract with a preservation architect, as smaller to medium-sized architecture firms typically do not staff that niche expertise full time.

Microbusinesses across many industries can garner advantages from this approach. The benefit to the client is that they do not have to engage a large firm, where costs could be much higher. In addition, partnering with microbusinesses can help prime contractors and owners meet their MWBE (Minority Women Business Enterprises) percentages, if applicable. Instead of having the contracts run parallel between service providers, they can run vertically to the prime or owner. Another benefit of this practice is that the firms become accustomed to working together—and with preestablished efficiencies, they can better serve the client and, ultimately, the project.

If you find yourself falling into the microbusiness definition, it may be to your advantage to seek out strategic alliances with service professionals and consultants who are consistently needed. A symbiotic relationship can bring new business to all participants, allowing you to grow your business more efficiently than what can be a slog of one job at a time and/or spending a lot on advertising with no guarantee of results.

Animals in the wild often work in groups for better efficiency and to thrive. It is no different among business owners. Identify and form alliances to achieve greater awareness and growth for your microbusiness.

Chapter 11

Celebrating a Personal Brand: Your Advocates

Whether you are a seasoned or emerging professional or embarking on a new small business venture, it is important to take stock of your advocates, those who will go to bat for you.

Advocates come in many different shapes and forms. They may be neighbors, professional colleagues, friends, family, or the coveted client/customer.

As opposed to a reference who willingly responds when asked, an advocate proactively sells you and your brand. When a prospect hears, "I know someone you should speak to," or "Let me put you in touch with someone I believe will help," from a trusted source who happens to be your advocate, it goes a long way. Sometimes, advocates appear when you least expect them. That is when you know you are truly making a positive difference in what you're doing.

We are all selling something. Whether it is a product, a service, intellectual property, or simply your ability to get a project done, we are all promoting something or someone. You can try to do it alone, but from your circle of trust to your extended acquaintances, why not enlist those who will support you in your quest?

Consider whom you advocate for. Is it reciprocal? If not, should you continue to advocate for them? Some people are naturally in a better position to advocate. It is surprising how much business is accomplished on a sporting field, at the gym, at your neighbor's house, or over a fence. The places are truly limitless.

Take stock of those around you. Identify those in a position to help promote your brand, reach out to them, and seek their support. If you are good at what you do, you can build a network of advocates who just might stumble across your next big project for you.

Make the most of your brand by identifying the people best suited to carry your flag. Your cadre of advocates can never be too broad or too expansive. It is indeed one aspect of your business that truly does not have any constraints.

Chapter 12

The Connectors

How often have you heard the phrase, "I got a guy for that"? We often need that "guy"—even if it is not a "guy" who ultimately helps us.

This is about being a connector, someone who knows a lot of people and has the relationships and resources to make it happen. For example, I once received a call from someone chairing a committee. They were seeking speakers for four events. The person was told to contact me because "I have connections." Well, I must say, that is true: I secured three speakers out of the four for them. And, I might add, I only knew two of them directly. I knew all three through my sister, perhaps one of the greatest connectors I know. Connections are all about linking to more and more people, not just an immediate colleague or friend.

In my corporate career, I was expected to be visible in the community, creating a high profile and personal brand. Since I am an extrovert, this was not a problem for me. In fact, I truly enjoyed setting up connections for clients—to suppliers, to potential customers, to a circle of trust advisors, to personal growth advisors. I feel satisfaction in knowing someone's life has been personally or professionally enriched because I helped them connect or made an introduction. When you think about it, as humans, it really is the least we can do for our friends, family, and colleagues.

So, who are these connectors? How do you find them and comfortably approach them? Let's identify them first. Look for higher-profile, outgoing, warm, and welcoming leaders. They may be the proverbial one degree of separation from you, perhaps known to a friend, family member, or colleague. Social media platforms like Facebook and LinkedIn are excellent for identifying who knows who. Also, a simple internet search may reveal articles or events with photos of your acquaintances and their acquaintances. One of those people may be your way into an introduction. Once you've identified them, ask for an introduction—meeting people and creating connections is part of their makeup and motivation.

Approaching connectors should not be difficult. In my example above, the person who contacted me about the speakers didn't know me personally. They did, however, know someone who had recently met me and identified me as someone with a lot of contacts—a good person to know for help. A simple email of introduction, and I was willing to assist.

The best way to approach a connector is with a warm introduction from another "connector." If you can't get a warm introduction, the next best option is a cold email or call. As mentioned, it is in their nature to expand their networks, so it is likely you will get some sort of response. If you can acquire their email address, I recommend sending a note of introduction first. If they don't respond after a few days, try a good old-fashioned phone call, again with a simple script of introduction: "Hi, my name is Xxxxx Xxxxx, I'm [state one brief interesting thing about you or your business], and I'd love to connect with you. I emailed you last week, so feel free to reply that way or call or text me at this number. Thanks!"

Connectors are everywhere: in our workplaces, our friendships, the small businesses we frequent, our clubs, our houses of worship, and our children's sports leagues. You get the idea. Take some time, do your research, use social media, and identify the connectors. Then, put an action plan in place to reach out to them and seek the help, guidance, and assistance you need or want. Speaking as one, I truly enjoy connecting people. I consider it a true compliment when I receive the type of communication I mentioned above. Just remember to thank them for their time and for their referral if they can make it for you. A written thank-you card is always a nice gesture in these electronic times. They will hopefully want to assist you again or as needed.

Reader challenge: Identify at least one connector in your life who can help you grow your business, refer the next great employee for your organization, or simply open a previously locked and impervious door. We all need co-pilots. Take your seat confidently and buckle up for an exciting ride.

Chapter 13

All in the Family

Your own family, human and canine, may evoke feelings of love, laughter, exasperation, and disappointment. With this chapter, I'm suggesting that often small businesses are family businesses, with many of the same joys and challenges that actual families have.

Recently, on a job site, a client mentioned that his recently retired father was now providing on-site maintenance. We laughed—and then realized that our consultant was a third-generation business. Brothers were working on our job, and my sister had hired me for business management on the job. We took a moment and clinked our water bottles in a toast to the family. They say it takes a village...but it really may take a family.

A majority of the companies I have worked with over the last twenty-five years have ownership with family ties. Throughout the office or plant, on the manufacturing floor, in the logistics department, or on the sales team, there would be siblings, spouses, parents, children, and in-laws. For most of them, this was a successful model. Would it work for you?

The advantages of working with family members can include instant trust, knowing what they do (and don't) bring to the proverbial table, and a feeling of ease and comfort in the familiar. Disadvantages may include taking liberties because they are family, bringing family issues to the office, and a blurred line between your personal life and your career. All of these should be considered when moving forward in a family-run business. However, my experience shows it seems to work more than it doesn't.

Remember, for the most part, your family should have the best interests of the company at heart. Trust in one another, treat each other with the same respect you would an unrelated colleague, and throw a party when you have successes to celebrate.

Protect your pack and have each other's back. Your synergy as a family team can provide the foundation to achieve more on the corporate side.

Chapter 14

Board Member Selection

A reader of my blog asked me to address the topic of board member selection. My experience sitting on several cultural boards, business advisory boards, and a healthcare board has allowed me to understand some of the challenges this board is currently encountering.

In my experience, a general description of a board of directors is a selective group of individuals who bring expertise or a mission-specific focus to the oversight of an organization. The organization can be a not-for-profit or a for-profit entity. Often, organizations like banks will have local community-based advisory boards to assist in the promotion and recommendation of a firm's local marketing efforts. Many small businesses have their circle of trusted professional advisors, but their advice comes with a price.

Small businesses may wish to consider an advisory board for their business. This is usually comprised of experts in areas that may assist small business owners in growing their businesses and raising their community profile. For this, the business owner would need to take the time to reach out to those experienced and well-known individuals they believe could advance their company. It takes resources and a keen sense to know what traits would benefit the firm. However, it can be very fruitful. For most advisory boards, the owner should be prepared to pay each member a nominal value for their time and expertise to assist them. While board membership at a non-profit is generally 100% volunteer, a business advisory board often is not.

The expertise selected for an advisory board may not be all that different from a traditional board of directors, managers, or trustees.

It's important for at least one of your board members to have a firm grasp of finance, financial statements, and financial analysis; most boards include at least one financial professional, such as a commercial banker. Their training in finance can be helpful in moving your business forward, especially if you anticipate requiring bank financing. Understanding how a bank perceives your industry and what type of financial and sales performance it expects is critical for growth and financing capital expenditures.

Selecting advisory board members should be in the best interest of the business or organization. At times, sports celebrities or well-known, accomplished family members may join boards to continue advocating for their personal causes or to support the small business or nonprofit in which they have taken a personal interest. Perhaps they are familiar with the owner. These types of board members can help raise the organization's profile as well as attract clients with their name recognition. Balancing this type of board member with a CPA, a banker, and an investment professional can be a viable strategy to achieve your business goals.

In addition to financial experts and community influencers, be sure to include subject matter experts—those with knowledge of your business service or product. If you are pursuing attorneys or bankers to join your advisory board, ask about their experience in your industry.

Many organizations will coalesce their boards with training and workshops. If you are interested in providing board governance training, seek out experts; the United Way has an excellent board training course that firms often use for their young professionals. It offers excellent content for preparing tomorrow's board members.

Remember, a board's advice is only as good as the experience of its members. If you have made wise choices regarding selection and ensured that you have a mix of financial expertise, market understanding, community representation, subject matter experts, and forward thinkers, be sure to provide them with a company orientation upon appointment. Such a board should be able to help your business exceed and excel.

Chapter 15

Expert Opinions

At times during the life cycle of a business, it is important to assess whether experts should be brought in to help market your product or service. Their roles can vary depending on the reasons for engaging them.

When I launched my firm's women's network, IWON, we initially augmented the meetings with confidential dialogue. We would then bring in an expert to expand on the topic we had just discussed among ourselves. It has been very well received. Identifying subject matter experts, or SMEs, as they are known in the trade, has been most beneficial. It adds an air of credibility to the topics being hashed out among the members. Additionally, it provides a new professional for us to, at minimum, network with and, if the need arises, to turn to in the future.

If a product or service you have or want to add has an uncertain reception or outcome, consider consulting with an SME, or you can always conduct a focus group with select clients or customers. Your existing client base is expert in the use of your product or service. Inviting them to be a part of a new launch will further bond them with your business and likely provide you with insights you may not have arrived at on your own.

Seeking other qualified opinions on any aspect of your business may both bring forth unexpected positive outcomes and provide that extra layer of credibility. Take it a step further and consider asking your SMEs to provide testimonials for your website and social media pages.

Section II: Points to Ponder

- Build a "circle of trust" advisor list; they will be your guiding support for the life of your business.
- Partner with other like-minded and complementary businesses; a team can be more impactful than just one player going it alone.
- Trade organizations and chambers of commerce can provide the much needed support a small business owner requires. Think of them as your handler out in the field. They may point you in the right direction when you least expect it.

Section III

Style

Business Branding

Another familiar saying that rings true for most of us is, "You only have one chance to make a first impression." How you or your business is viewed (or how your dog looks in its first performance) is a one-time opportunity. Make it count.

In this section, read about the many facets of that first impression, from your logo to the marketing surrounding it. Brand it with your signature style.

Chapter 16

Your Brand, Your Image

Your personal identity or brand may be very different from the professional image or brand you wish to convey to clients. Budding entrepreneurs need to give this concept serious thought.

First, ask yourself, "What is my current personal brand?" If you are unsure, ask your closest friends and family members. Are you seen as introverted or happy-go-lucky? Or are you a chameleon, adaptable and comfortable in any situation? See what rings true to you, and then turn to who you want to be professionally.

Your professional brand image should be clear and concise. Start with defining what you need to convey to your client base to ensure sales will follow. Come up with at least three words that you will use as your firm's brand objective. Perhaps "quality," "decisive," and "expert," for example. You wish to convey to clients and potential clients that you deliver a *quality* product or service, you are *decisive* in your business decisions, and you are an *expert* in the firm's field. These can serve as a foundation from which to build the image you want staring back at you professionally.

Second, work with your brand marketing advisor. This is an important opportunity for your logo to reflect your company goals and values that you used to define the professional image you are ultimately seeking. Remember, we talked about the value of a graphic designer as well. Branding professionals have experience drawing out information from their clients, which in this case is you. They elicit ideas about the "personality" of your vision for your brand. While not all of us have a sense of design, you may have thoughts about, for example, the colors of your business logo. I researched logo colors and found that yellow was one of the least used. I wanted to portray a guiding light in my effort to convey my field of consulting. I have always been fascinated by lanterns and found an image in a catalog selling various types of lanterns. I presented that to my brand manager and asked her to create a logo with that in mind. Trust your designer and give input where you can. Work with them to tell your story the way you want it told.

The name of your business is one of the most important aspects of your business that you will ever create. Make sure it reflects you and your business effort, and that it sparks an interest in your product or service. Most importantly, let it reflect what you hope others will think of when they hear or see it. You may also need to consult with your attorney. The right one will have experience with copyright law and help you check with your state business name domain to see if it is available. This is an important step; if you go ahead with a name or look that is already copyrighted, it could cause a lot of problems down the road. I also recommend running some of your top choices by those who know you best. Their insight can help confirm that the name truly fits who you are and what you are selling or making. When you are comfortable that you have a winning name that is legally available, move forward.

Remember, your company is about you at the core. Exuding a positive image of the goods or services you are selling will be a winning combination. Check in with yourself to ensure you understand the correct professional image you need to project to make your company and its brand effective and attractive to your prospective client base.

Chapter 17

Speak Up

There are many ways to market your personal brand and your business together. One of the most common methods is to accept speaking engagements about yourself and your business.

Chambers of Commerce often present seminars on aspects of a business that apply to everyone. Examples include banking, legal advice, investments, cash management, supply chain management, logistics management, etc. The list can go on and on. If you belong to a chamber, it is worth investigating whether there are any opportunities that make sense for you to offer a free presentation on your business. Do not be afraid to make the inquiry; you never know what may come out of the effort!

Another great venue for you to market your brand is a professional trade association. Depending on your service or product, consider trade associations in manufacturing or the medical, dental, veterinary, legal, architecture, accounting, or engineering communities. All of these professions require annual continuing education credits, and perhaps your presentation can qualify.

Don't overlook clubs where members could utilize your service. Research business and social clubs in your area. Your talk may be just what they have been searching for.

Additionally, not-for-profits whose missions may benefit from your offerings can be a good source of marketing for you. Gaining awareness of organizations like these can help propel your personal brand, your corporate brand, or both. Sometimes, the simplest of gathering places yield great results.

Assess whether incorporating speaking engagements makes sense for you and your organization. Professionals who offer to give a talk to an organization are de facto networking, whether they speak about their business or use their expertise to demonstrate why their listeners should be interested. If nothing else, it should encourage dialogue around you and your business offerings. And free positive marketing is always welcome.

Find ways to present your story. Certainly, there is an audience out there that will benefit from what you have to say.

Chapter 18

Grab That Award

Local business associations, business papers, and chambers of commerce often solicit or provide nominations and awards for business excellence. This is another opportunity for you and your brand to garner a higher profile.

With themes like "Thirty under Thirty," "Forty under Forty," business leadership and influence awards, project awards, professional achievement awards, and more, there may be an area where you or your company can stand out from your competition. The key is to identify which awards you believe you qualify for and how best to position yourself to achieve one.

First, look at your chamber of commerce and your local business newspaper. These organizations almost always provide or solicit nominations or awards in a variety of categories. Some additional categories you might see are women- or minority-related success and company milestone–related success. If you take the time to look, there should be a category for which you qualify.

These types of business community awards are generally "pay to play." That means you need to join the local business association that sponsors and/or creates the awards. You need to subscribe to the newspaper that compiles the lists of the most influential or most powerful business leaders. If you don't, it is often an unspoken barrier to entry. These nominations are strategic in nature and often promote the sponsors as much as the winners.

However, having been a recipient of one of these awards, it is a moment to savor. The ceremony, the public relations, the advertising and subsequent news write-up, and the photo—don't forget the photo! The image and press surrounding your moment of fame are both a celebration of effort and a profile of achievement. It is advertising, and it is a statement that you, your company, or both, have been identified as rising above the competition. It can propel your brand to the next level.

So, join that chamber, subscribe to that journal, and participate in your local business community. Research the qualifications, and when you believe you or your firm's accomplishments have met the requirements, apply, nominate, and target that award. The media, the celebration luncheon, the article in the paper, and the physical plaque to display on your office wall—each of these represents a marketing and social media opportunity and a moment to rise above your industry competitors.

Going the extra mile to participate in strategic organizations can result in a boost to your leadership profile. Go for the award that best celebrates your professional and community accomplishments. It feels good to be recognized, applauded, and celebrated. We all deserve a bit of fame for our hard work and contributions. Go find yours!

Chapter 19

Making a Splash With Your Signage

I am always fascinated by the types of signage businesses choose to convey their brand. There are so many choices, and yet only that one chance to make the right first impression.

When it comes to exterior signage, it certainly can be effective to stick with your logo. Keep the brand message consistent, and select a material that enhances the visual message, such as stone, wood, or metal. And there is always flashing neon. Consult a professional company that can advise you on how best to iterate your intended design.

Zoning is another important aspect. There are limits and requirements regarding the type of exterior signage in any municipality. A good sign company will know what those are. If you are in a historically significant location, there may be additional guidelines.

With so many types of signs, make sure you choose the one that best reflects you and your company. It is a message to the world about who or what is behind the door.

Make it count. Make it significant. Make it consistent. Let it tell your story for you.

Chapter 20

Choosing the Right Domain Name

One of the trickiest aspects of starting your business can be choosing the right domain name for your website. If you thought coming up with the company name was hard, wait until you need to finalize the domain name.

In the United States, most domain names end with .com. There are alternatives, such as .net, .org, or .co. For our friends in Canada, the domain names usually end in .ca. How do you choose which is right for your business? And is there an advantage of one over the other? These are must-ask questions for your brand manager among your advisors.

Like any important aspect of your business, choosing a domain name requires research. If you search "domain name lookup," you will find several options to input the name or names you are considering. And does the name matter? Depending on the industry, it may be more important than in others. I find it confusing when I am looking up a retail establishment, say a hotel, and I cannot find its domain where one would think it would be, under the name of the business. Hotels will often be under an unfamiliar corporate parent name. Small business retail shops may be under their names or, if their exact name was not available, it may be a derivative. I often find that I need to check their social media and hope they have a direct link there to their website.

For non-retail businesses, you will see a variety of domain names. Some may describe the product or service or be under a catchphrase that fits the business or its products and services. For my own business, "Illuminate" was already taken. This is when decisions become very consequential. I ended up shortening "Business Consulting" to BC in my domain name. In retrospect, I believe I should have spelled out the entire name. This would have alleviated confusion with similarly named businesses. The good news is if you choose to "transfer" your domain name, a good website developer will be able to work with your domain provider, such as GoDaddy, and limit the difficulties such a switch can create.

The concept of purchasing like-named domains is something you will also need to consider when you register yours. Some people buy up similar names, perhaps the .net and .org versions of your name, to try and ward off the competition. After all, the point is to drive traffic to your website, not anyone else's, let alone a competitor's. You may also consider whether to copyright your business name. And, if so, which countries to copyright it in. The risk of others using a similar name is real; you should take caution in choosing the domain name. Consult with your brand manager and your attorney. Most common words, by their very definition, cannot be copyrighted. So, in my case, while "illuminate" is a common word, many of the firms are in different industries. For that reason, I did not have to worry about impinging upon someone else's copyright by using that word.

If you work with your trusted advisors on the creation and do your research, hopefully you will be able to create a domain name that supports your brand, advertises your brand, is easy for customers or clients to locate, and is easily remembered. This is not a simple process. It should be treated with the same care you treated your business name, to minimize any reputation risk you might suffer from ending up with a domain name that is not suited to your business or is associated with another company.

If you do it right, your domain name easily reflects or relates to your business name.

Chapter 21

Mentor Me, Mentor You

In any industry, for any position, there can be mentors. In fact, structured or unstructured mentorship can lead you to a pathway of success and will certainly augment your brand.

Mentorship comes in many forms. In many larger organizations, there are structured mentorship programs. Employees can apply for both the mentor and mentee positions. Not everyone who applies is chosen; there has to be a good fit between the two. These programs are largely run through the company's human resources division. They run for specific time intervals with checkpoints for progress, and there is accountability on both sides.

A more organic or unstructured mentorship may be part of a manager's or leader's role. At times, these relationships develop out of synergistic flows between colleagues at various levels or in divergent specialty areas. An employee can voice interest in someone else's role and take time to research, question, and shadow to learn as much as possible. Not every leader is willing to unofficially mentor, and some may not have the time. Identifying the right mentor is as critical as identifying the area in which you want to learn more.

I have been on both sides of the mentor role in my corporate career. My first boss took me under his wing and helped me learn many aspects of commercial relationship banking. He was critical to my success. I am forever thankful to him for his time, patience, insight, and willingness to share.

As a result, any time I came across a colleague who wanted to know more, to learn more, to be more, it was important to me to help them in any way I could. I had that opportunity with at least several younger colleagues. All are very successful and have made, and continue to make, their mark in the banking community. I am very proud of them and feel privileged to have been a cog in their wheel of success.

You can never stop learning. I believe that mentoring is very fulfilling and can also provide lifelong benefits. The desire to help others is an attribute that will circulate in your community, strengthening your brand as an expert in your field and as someone willing to pass on that expertise to those who are coming up around you.

Always be on the lookout to learn or to teach. Your career path may provide many opportunities to be a follower or a leader. Your personal brand can benefit from both.

Section III: Points to Ponder

- You only have one opportunity to make a first impression with your firm's brand and identity; make it count.
- Add a graphic designer with branding experience to your circle of trusted advisors. They will be the painter in your work of art, your business.
- Establish yourself as an expert through mentoring in your field. Such efforts will strengthen your brand and enhance your profile as a leader.

Section IV

Movement & Mechanics

Required Business Tools

In any game, a fundamental understanding of the core principles, those that make up an operating system, should be studied, orchestrated with great precision, and focused on an ultimate goal or achievement.

In dog field work, that core understanding is usually the ultimate target. In the business world, it is your firm's success. How best to achieve that and what fundamentals are necessary for that success are included in this section of business commentary. You will explore everything from a good video conference system to an insurance policy for "your pack" to help keep your operation balanced!

- Chapter 22: Certified Business Enterprises – Differentiate Yourself on the Field
- Chapter 23: Unlocking the Mystery of Your NAICS Code
- Chapter 24: Are You Invisible to Your Bank?
- Chapter 25: Insuring Your Pack
- Chapter 26: Business Incentives – Treat Yourself
- Chapter 27: Navigating Contracts
- Chapter 28: On the Hunt for a Notary
- Chapter 29: Voom With a View
- Chapter 30: Somewhere Over the Rainbow (Drone Technology)

Chapter 22

Certified Business Enterprises – Differentiate Yourself on the Field

Let's face it, no matter the industry, it's a "dog-eat-dog" world. Competition is fierce. So, what can you do to differentiate yourself?

For those of us who meet the qualifications of one or more certified business enterprises (CBEs), this marketing tool can be a distinct competitive advantage. It is worth the time and financial resources required to complete the certification process if you qualify for any of the following common CBEs:

- Women Business Enterprise (WBE)
- Minority Business Enterprise (MBE)
- Veteran Business Enterprise (VBE)
- Disadvantaged Business Enterprise (DBE)
- Disability Owned Business Enterprise (DOBE)

It is important to note that certification for any of these usually has to be done at the federal, state, county, and city levels. Some counties and cities combine for one application, but I have not seen any at the state level that can be used in lieu of the federal level or the county/city level. Why? It is unknown, frankly. As a small business owner, it is one more administrative task that you can either take on yourself or outsource to your business consultant, attorney, or perhaps your CPA. Fair warning—we have heard one manufacturing owner describe the process as "intrusive." And it is. The governing bodies need to ensure that applicants qualify on their merit and that the required data is complete. The certification also needs to be updated regularly, which means you must constantly reapply. After all, certification is a privilege, so weave it into your normal annual budget for both time and money.

The most important component for all of these certifications is that the primary owner, responsible for the company's operations, must own 51% or more of the company. Applicants must show forms of eligibility proving that they both own 51% and that their expertise is indispensable to the company's operation. The VBE and the DOBE have additional paperwork requirements, and the DBE is a financial litmus test. The DBE is applicable to Department of Transportation projects and is attained through an in-depth financial review and a threshold that must be met.

There are also additional certifications available to WBE and MBE firms, including HubZone, 8(a), and WOSB (Women Owned Small Business). Often, military organizations prioritize working with VBEs, given their close affiliation. It is a wonderful perk associated with recognizing the sacrifices veterans have made on the country's behalf. Each state sets its minimum requirement for the percentage of work that needs to be contracted to CBEs; they are all not the same. The DBE has its own contract percentage set by the secretary of transportation. The percentage may also be set at the project CBE level as well. But do not be overwhelmed; if you can qualify for this work, it is often a steady, life-long income stream and worth all the effort.

The biggest advantage is when a project you are bidding for uses government funding, which requires a certain percentage of the project to be allocated among CBEs. Knowing the source of the funding for any given project is your best entry into determining if your CBE will be useful. Privately funded projects are not usually subject to these same percentage requirements for CBEs.

If you believe your business could benefit from one or more of these designations, take the time to either read up on them or seek professional consultation. You never know what work may be just around the corner, and it may be worth your time to secure one of these to stand out among your competitors.

Chapter 23

Unlocking the Mystery of Your NAICS Code

The world is filled with acronyms. One that you will often hear when you own your own business is the NAICS code.

NAICS stands for North American Industry Classification System. A NAICS (pronounced "nakes") code is a classification within the North American Industry Classification System. The NAICS system was developed for use by Federal Statistical Agencies for the collection, analysis, and publication of statistical data related to the U.S. economy. It is used by the United States, Canada, and Mexico to classify businesses by industry. Every business, upon formation, must be classified into a six-digit NAICS code based on the majority of business conducted. This is an essential element of your legal formation, and you will need it at various times throughout the life of your business.

Upon formation of your company, unless you are a sole proprietor not electing to use a DBA, you will need to self-classify your business's NAICS code, as it will be needed to obtain your EIN (Employer Identification Number). You can find the list of over 1,000 NAICS codes online at www.naics.com. Choose the one that most closely resembles your primary service or product. If you have questions about the best fit, your attorney or accountant can be consulted for assistance. Since the IRS requires the NAICS code for federal tax submissions, it is always preferable to clear your choice with your accountant before you apply for the EIN.

You may wonder why is this important. Well, there are a number of reasons why a correct NAICS is important for a business. First, the IRS requires it for your federal tax return. Second, it is used by banks for assessing risk tolerance. There are many high-risk and prohibited NAICS codes identified by banks for commercial underwriting purposes. Some examples may be adult video stores, cannabis stores or manufacturers, spec buildings, money service businesses, collection agencies, and investment real estate. This list varies by bank, so before you assume your bank is interested in your business, you should clear your assigned NAICS Code with them. There is a detailed list of commonly considered high-risk NAICS codes on the website mentioned above.

If you seek financing for your company, the bank will ask for your NAICS code. A particular bank may not have a current appetite for your code; perhaps their portfolio is weighted too heavily in that industry. Alternatively, it may require a special credit group within the bank that has the knowledge and experience in that industry. Oil and gas is a great example. Certain NAICS codes and industries are so specific that banks hire and train personnel to understand and work with those businesses only. In theory, this should assist you, as the bank specialist should truly understand the nuances of your industry.

NAICS codes are also required if you are applying for any type of government contract work or if you apply for a women/minority/small business/disadvantaged/veteran certification. Some contracts require firms to be in specific NAICS codes. You will also be required to register with the various government agencies in their bidding systems; the NAICS code is required to be a part of that database. Other corporations or government agencies, like FEMA, may search by NAICS code for vendors needed on projects. Therefore, it is important that you self-classify correctly. Otherwise, you could presumably be excluded from potential vendor searches.

Besides your actual EIN (Employer Identification Number, akin to an individual's SSN), the NAICS code is an important number to keep handy. It is also a good research locator if you are trying to access specific industry information online. You will be surprised at how much information you can acquire on your chosen NAICS code.

So, be informed, be aware, and unlock the mystery of your code. As always, information is power, and you should access as much as possible to help your business grow and thrive.

Chapter 24

Are You Invisible to Your Bank?

If you do not have an assigned relationship manager looking out for your business at your bank, you need to ask yourself: "Have I become invisible to my bank?" A dialogue about how to establish a friendlier, open channel of communication with your bank is a must.

As a commercial banker for most of my corporate career, I encountered a variety of business types, spanning the spectrum of personalities among their owners. Shaping my own behavior to work with, advocate for, and educate each one took the majority of my time over the years. For the most part, I was successful in achieving open and friendly relationships with my clients. However, even in more challenging discussions, respect was the most important aspect of our communication. Indeed, it saw us through the Great Recession, and I imagine it is helping my previous clients with their current assigned bank representatives today.

You may ask, "What can a small or microbusiness do to improve its relationship with its bank?" Despite not having an assigned bank rep and/or a small amount on deposit with your bank, it can be done. Choose your business bank wisely. And, regardless of the extent of the financial relationship, remember you are still their customer.

Here are some of the steps I found particularly helpful as a microbusiness when I decided to embark on the Illuminate Business Consulting journey:

1) Choose a bank that suits your financial needs. Ideally, this bank has a physical banking center nearby where you can become acquainted with the staff and, most importantly, the banking center manager.

2) Forge a personal financial relationship with the bank. Some ideas include opening a personal deposit checking and/or savings account, adding personal overdraft protection, a personal rewards credit card, or a home equity line of credit (HELOC), refinance or take out a new automobile loan. If there are any additional personal products you can use, try to open them with your business bank.

On the business account side, always ask your bank for a quote or proposal on merchant credit card processing (where your business accepts credit cards). Look to share milestones with your local bank, such as an anniversary or a financial statement update. As your business grows, you will need more products and additional services.

The more products you have with a bank, whether on the individual or business side, the better. In the trade, it is referred to as "share of wallet." If you know your business will not have the big dollars to garner unsolicited attention, you can easily compensate by making every effort to allow the bank to profit from your financial dealings, no matter how big or how small. It makes a difference.

3) Open up your business account in person, not online. Some banks do not allow you to open new accounts over the Internet .This is a quick way to ensure your anonymity. That may work until something like a pandemic comes along. Then, knowing your local banker will be a valuable asset.

4) If your account has been in existence for a while, you can always improve your relationship with your bank by simply walking into the closest branch. Exchange pleasantries with the staff; perhaps even ask to meet the manager just to introduce yourself. All banks operating in the U.S. are normally bound by the Patriot Act and its requirement to "Know Your Customer," so an in-person introduction, regardless of the reason, helps both parties get to know one another.

5) Perhaps the most important step is to "stay in touch." As simple as that sounds, it is easy to go months without real contact with your local banking center. Do not let this happen. Send them a thank you or holiday card, at a minimum, for the help they have given

you, even if you haven't needed a lot. You can also post a social media review—Yelp, Yahoo, Facebook, comment about the friendly service, or if you are on LinkedIn, search for your branch manager and connect with them. Consider posting a photo of the branch on Instagram and tagging the institution. If your banking center manager is willing to give you their business card, it likely includes their direct email address. Take advantage of that, and use it to keep in communication. Use all these channels available to you, whichever you are most comfortable with, but DO stay in touch.

6) The final, and perhaps the most important, aspect is to "be visible" to your bank. If your local branch participates in any volunteer efforts, such as collecting nonperishable items for a local food bank, toys or school supplies for children, or flowers for hospice, *be visible* and participate in whichever of these efforts suits your engagement with your bank.

Employing some or all of these behaviors is how Illuminate stays in touch with our local community bank.

Please learn from my unique perspective, both as a commercial banker and as a small business owner. You do not have to be invisible to your bank because your small or microbusiness funds are not eye-catching to them. Forging a working relationship with your bank makes it much more likely that the next time you need assistance with an overdraft refund, a new check register, or a disaster loan when a global pandemic occurs, they will be there to guide you.

Chapter 25

Insuring Your Pack

You have your own business. Now, what, as it relates to health insurance? Do you need to cover yourself, or can you utilize a family member's plan? Should the plan be just for yourself, or should it cover your "pack" as well? These are a few of the questions a small business owner needs to ask themselves, at a minimum, upon opening and annually thereafter.

If you have employees, the most common method of handling this part of a business is working through a licensed insurance agent. My experience has found clients using their agent for anywhere from five to 1,000 employees. From doing the groundwork for you to receiving reduced rates based on their experience, contacts, and knowledge, using an agent takes a large part of the burden off you. The agent adds a commission fee to the price, but it is likely worth it.

The next most common approach is to use the HR offerings of your firm's payroll agent. Ask if they have HR functions, which include negotiating and setting up healthcare options. This seems to be the preferred option for businesses with one to five employees, in my experience.

The wild card is your local chamber of commerce. Many offer this service. Usually, a licensed insurance agent on staff at your chamber will work with you directly on details such as the number of employees, their scope of work, what percentage of contribution you want to cover, years in service, industry, etc. Many factors drive the risk and the pool they are able to group your company into. The more firms in the pool, usually the lower the cost to each employer. The larger chambers require a minimum number of employees, generally two or more, to include your company in this offering. Chambers that target small businesses often have the most competitive plans available for sole proprietors, something to be cognizant of when you call for a quote.

In many ways, your local chamber acts as the insurance broker, similar to your own insurance agent. It makes sense to consider their offerings. If you do not have a business consultant, office manager, or accountant willing to gather all the paperwork to solicit multiple quotes from chambers, insurance agencies, and third-party brokers, it is worth your money to pay a circle of trust advisor to take on this project.

It has been our experience that organization leaders felt the "security in numbers" offered by an insurance agent or a chamber provided less stress on the individual company and provided the best options.

The analysis of health insurance is one of the most intense components of business evolution, and it should be given proper time for research and analysis. Much like dogs, no two are ever alike, and you may need to consider how much you and your business are willing to invest in this employee benefit.

Understand your budget, formulate a clear plan regarding health insurance for yourself as the owner and for your employees, and investigate your options thoroughly on how to best keep your "pack" healthy and safe.

Chapter 26

Business Incentives – Treat Yourself

In the dog training world, positive reinforcement training consists of treating or rewarding your dog to achieve good or desired behavior, as opposed to punishing bad behavior. So, can you apply this same behavior to your business? Absolutely!

Government and Quasi-Government Organizations, most notably industrial development agencies, or IDAs, as they are commonly known, provide incentives (or treats) to businesses for good behavior. If you are planning to relocate, build, expand, or purchase equipment and you are going to hire more employees (all good behaviors), you will want to speak to your local IDA! These are the exact behaviors they wish to reward businesses for, as they're essential to economic stability and growth. Their "treats" come in various forms—from property tax abatement to sales tax waivers to cost of power reductions. Each governing IDA has its own bag of treats to offer, and none are the same as others. So, it is imperative to contact the governing IDA in the physical geography where your business is located or will be located.

There are some caveats, of course. IDA incentives do not normally apply to retail or professional services firms. However, if you are one of the certified disadvantaged enterprise businesses (WBE, MBE, DBE, etc.) and you are a retailer or offer professional services, there may be exclusions in your local IDA regulations. It is also important to note that the less urban IDAs seem to have more flexibility with the types of businesses they work with.

You can normally identify your local IDA by asking your business consultant, lawyer, banker, or accountant, or through an internet search. So, for your next expansion, equipment purchase, acquisition, or hiring phase, be sure to investigate how your local Industrial Development Agency may be able to help.

Chapter 27

Navigating Contracts

For most professional-type services, particularly start-ups or those entering a new source of revenue, the prospect of negotiating contracts can be daunting. But rest assured, there is help!

Business owners have options when entering contracts for services with prospective clients. The first, and likely the least risky, is to use an attorney—perhaps the same attorney you have in your circle of trust. Most attorneys who specialize in business matters have the expertise to create your legal entity and assist you with contract negotiation. Yes, you will need to pay them, but the investment will likely reduce any related anxiety, resulting in peace of mind. It is important to remember that attorneys carry malpractice insurance, and that alone should be worth engaging them.

Choosing an attorney is an important step in the evolution of your business. As we mentioned in the section on developing your circle of trust earlier in the book, your attorney should have synergy with you and understand your business or at least its goals. Dare you call them a friend? Often, close legal advisors like your accountant and your banker will become more than business consultants. It is imperative that you are comfortable with them as individuals, as well as with the leader of their firm, and confident in its reputation. You must also value their input and feel that their fees are appropriate. An attorney who does not share your moral compass, your political views, or your social concerns may end up being a source of frustration and anxiety. Keep in mind that the most expensive attorney isn't necessarily the ideal legal advisor for you.

Illuminate sourced several legal advisors. Our long-time attorney had just been elected to a judgeship, so she could no longer provide legal services. We then worked with an online legal formation service; one we had used in a prior business. Their services include following up on annual filings, which is helpful. However, we soon realized we required a local attorney to assist with matters like liability counsel and contract negotiation. It is likely one of the best decisions we made. Additionally, we do call our attorney "friend" as well. We begin each workweek with great confidence, knowing our back is covered from a legal counsel standpoint.

Your other choice is to go it alone without legal counsel. Many professionals rely on their professional liability insurance agent to help guide them on the proper forms required for their certification. This is essential for many professionals, but it does not provide the additional layer of legal coverage that an attorney would. In an ideal situation, your firm would work with both your professional liability insurance agent and your legal counsel. Often, they may need to dialogue directly as well. So, if you are without legal representation on your letters of agreement or your sub-consultant contracts, you are exposing your firm, and perhaps yourself as an individual, to greater risk. Think hard about this as you conduct business. As your contracts become more complicated or the revenue at stake is more impactful, having a legal eye to oversee this aspect of your business is a wise path to choose.

Remember to identify options and interview several candidates to see who is the best fit, both on a personal level and from an expertise perspective. With the right legal support, you can grow your business wisely and with a lesser degree of risk, which is always a positive move for any company. If you are unsure whom to interview, ask your fellow business owners, your accountant, your friends, or your family for recommendations. That is how we assembled our list to speak with at formation, and we could not be happier with how it worked out with our chosen legal counsel. An endorsement from a trusted colleague, friend, or family member goes a long way in this search.

So, think wisely before you navigate any new surroundings. Your contract will dictate how you proceed, and a qualified legal advisor can help provide you with the life raft you may need to get across to the other side.

Chapter 28

On the Hunt for a Notary

Certifications, such as a WBE, are often renewed annually. While the information for a straight renewal may not be consequential, it turns out that the search for a notary may be!

Pre-pandemic, most banking centers, open daily, had a notary on staff. Now, visits to banking centers may require appointments to meet with anyone other than a teller. This means that finding a notary, which should not be a struggle, is not as simple as it once was. If and when you are looking for one, start with your bank. Call to confirm if and when a notary will be available, and then book an appointment.

If your bank can't help with this, the next logical location would be an attorney's office. In New York State, most attorneys are also notaries. However, in these post-pandemic times, attorneys are not always in their offices. Much like the trip to the bank, it requires phone calls or emails to confirm when a notary can be available.

AAA and UPS offer notary services. However, be aware of limitations. Certain membership levels with AAA may require a fee for notarization. Our experience with UPS, which was very convenient, included a minimum fee. For these options, make sure you confirm that the location you are heading to has a notary available. A phone call and appointment are often recommended and/or required.

If your business is located in a commercial building, check with the administrative office or other tenants. There may be one in the building! After I experienced the convenience of UPS, I discovered that was the case at our location.

There's no doubt that, at some point, you will need a notary. So, instead of digging yourself into a hole like that dog hunting a small critter tunnel, explore your options and save yourself some time.

Chapter 29

Voom With a View

With the cultural shift from in-person to video-based meetings, a disturbing trend seems to be emerging. With no rules governing such calls, each participant is left to create his or her own view and application. While flexibility is key to this approach, there are some guidelines we all should follow.

First and foremost, if you are invited to what I like to refer to as "voom" calls, "v" emphasizing *video*, make sure you can join *with video* enabled. The meeting organizer likely selected video so that the participants can see each other to try and approximate the historically acceptable method of in-person meetings. The same protocols should apply whether the meeting is held in person or via video. Without video, the call can be choppy, distracting, and likely not effective.

There may be legitimate reasons why some attendees cannot join the call with video. They may be on the road or experiencing technical issues. If this is you, please do the polite thing and inform your host or organizer that, regretfully, you cannot join by video and provide the reason. This can be shared with the broader group so everyone understands why all they see is a phone number next to your name.

Secondly, if you are the host, ask yourself why the meeting is arranged as a Voom call. Do you have visuals that need to be shared with and viewed by the group? Or are you just feeling the burden of isolation and wanting to see the participants? If half of the participants opt not to turn their cameras on, it is likely that this is not the best time for a meeting, or they do not believe a video connection is warranted. As the organizer, you may have to rethink the timing and choice of communication for your meeting. Perhaps a good old-fashioned teleconference is sufficient and free of these distractions.

I experienced just this situation recently, and I was left wondering why others didn't want us to see them. It was both distracting and rude. We all need to adapt to this altered business culture, and doing your best to maintain decorum and protocol should be a priority for all.

So, the next "Voom" meeting you are invited to, consider that the host or organizer has asked you to be truly present. For those of us who have taken the time to raise the computer to eye level, as is best practice, or have arranged an appealing background, please extend us the same courtesy. We do not want to see you in your bathrobe meandering through the refrigerator. Assuming you are not having technology connection issues, join the video. Stage yourself for an appealing view for your colleagues. It really is the least we all can do for one another in this new approach to business.

Chapter 30

Somewhere Over the Rainbow (Drone Technology)

When it is time to add a different perspective to running your business, there is no need to take a step forward or backward; just look up. And somewhere over that rainbow, you may hear the buzzing of the future—a drone.

One of our clients purchased a drone and used it to photograph the top of a building built in the 1800s for a project of theirs. The results were amazing. Even though some of us had climbed up the narrow steps and crawled through the small attic space to have a look at the roof, nothing could have prepared us for the awe-inspiring views from the sky. The client is using them to analyze the cause of some of the issues with the aging building. There is nothing like a top-down view. It truly gives you perspective, literally and figuratively.

According to Datafloq.com, the drone industry is expected to reach $100 billion in the next few years. Opportunities appear to be vast and ever-growing. They list the following seven areas of growth: retail, transportation, entertainment, agriculture, search & rescue, home security, and construction. Our use falls in the last category.

When it comes time to spice up your marketing material, consider drone photography of your business or highlight the use of drone photography on a project. It is a clear way to differentiate your services and will garner attention. Many commercial photographers are offering drone photos. This approach is likely a more affordable way to see what drone technology can do for your business before investing in one yourself.

New technology is always exciting, and drones are no exception. Being able to soar above your normal views can give you a renewed sense of excitement about how your business can be perceived. Showcasing a different side of you, your services, your products, or your actual location can help you achieve an immediate positive impact. If you are a commercial mural artist, a manufacturer, or a professional service provider, there is always a different view to that next project.

Look to find a new perspective – over the rainbow. It may be time to click those proverbial ruby shoes and take your business to a new level. A fresh, top-down view can be your own yellow brick road.

Section IV: Points to Ponder

- Be aware of how the government classifies you – Certified Business Entities, NAICS code – and make sure you are a recognizable business to your bank of choice.
- Understand all the operational aspects of running your business, from a proper video conference setup to drone technology to navigating legal contracts to insuring your organization. All these components are essential for operating at maximum efficiency.

Section V

The Perfect Crate

Office Space & Real Estate

If you have ever been around canine sports or working arenas, you will have noticed the creativity surrounding the personal space for the dogs. There are logos, there are blankets, there are gorgeous fabrics, and so many varieties of what makes up the dog's "home away from home"—their crate.

Creating office space is no different. Finding and making that space your own creates your physical brand image and needs to be a place of inspiration and practicality for your products and/or services. This section addresses the importance of finding and creating your perfect office space and real estate.

- Chapter 31: Location, Location, Location
- Chapter 32: Pointing Towards Churches for Office Space
- Chapter 33: Taking the Leap – Commercial Office Space vs. Home Office
- Chapter 34: Staring Down a Lease
- Chapter 35: Ground-Up Construction
- Chapter 36: Protecting Your Office Space
- Chapter 37: Mates in Their Crates
- Chapter 38: Office Critter Control

Chapter 31

Location, Location, Location

Locating a building that both allows you to succeed and reflects your business image is among the most important decisions you make that impact the future welfare of your company. Recently, for varied clients, we looked at multiple locations, from warehouse and industrial spaces to storefronts to converted churches. This has prompted the question: How does a business owner choose the right location for their business? Is cheaper always better?

Clearly, the first step is to work with a commercial realtor whom you trust and who understands your geographic market. If you do not know any realtors, ask your circle of trusted advisors to recommend some for you to consider. They need to have experience and knowledge of both your industry and your competitive market. Ideally, they should also have the right connections with other established realtors. If you end up in a bidding war, will your realtor's relationship with the seller's realtor hurt or hinder your chances of winning? Having a realtor as a trusted advisor helps mitigate what can be an overwhelming time. It should allow you to focus on the most important question: Is this the right location and the right building for my brand?

Second, research the neighborhood. If the perfect building is in the wrong location, this may catch up with you. You know your business best, and you know where it needs to be to flourish. This is most important for retail or professional firms. Clients or customers need to be able to access you at their convenience, not yours. Keep that in mind when evaluating a location, and be on the lookout for things such as public transportation, free parking, and ease of ingress/egress.

If the surrounding neighborhood does not reflect your clientele, will they want to visit you there? Or does the neighborhood present new opportunities to expand or change your clientele? You are moving for a reason. Is this location reflective of that reason?

And last but certainly not least, does the location feel right to you if you are to become its proprietor? Karma, feeling bonded to your location, can work wonders for a positive and inspiring work environment. Does it face south and receive sunlight? Are there enough windows? Is it welcoming? And certainly, do not underestimate the importance of decorating your place of business in the colors that reflect your passion for your work. A happy owner is usually a successful owner. Before you make your decision, stand out in front of the location and look around. If that makes you smile and gives you a sense of pride, it may be the right place to start a new journey. If it creates confusion, it may be time to rethink this location and keep looking. Trust yourself to know your brand, where it can excel, and where it may be washed away within the view. Make this evaluation in the sunlight; a dreary weather day can alter the location's true impact.

At the end of the day, you need to relax and enjoy your space, but above all, you need to be able to afford the location. Let it reflect who you are and make it work in your favor. There is no need to oversell yourself on affording a building that really is not within your budget. From day one, it's likely that your clients will sense your anxiety about whether you made the right decision. Find a compromise between what you can afford and the ideal location. Often, location can be as much a mindset as it is an actual address.

Location, location, location has merit when it comes to embracing your brand image and setting yourself up for future success. Put your personal stamp on your spot, relish the impact it makes in your neighborhood, and sustainably project a proud and vibrant image; your clients and your neighbors will surely take notice!

Chapter 32

Pointing Towards Churches for Office Space

Have you ever noticed that GOD spelled backward is DOG? Coincidence? I, like many dog owners, believe not.

Recently, it was brought to my attention that churches can be great opportunities for reasonable office space for small businesses. A member of our women's idea exchange network gave us a tour of her office in a glorious historic church. It was bright, spacious, and truly felt like a small community.

One of our first articles centered around commercial leases. It seems that the church offerings may provide an ideal situation for a small business owner or solopreneur. Frequently, utilities and Wi-Fi are included. There is usually a fee for parking, but the dreaded triple net lease is generally not an issue. And that is something to celebrate as a tenant!

Some of the amenities offered in well-cared-for historic churches are high ceilings, gorgeous historic doorways, stained glass windows, and detailed crown molding. The feeling of tranquility was perhaps the most impressive part of my tour. It had me thinking that if Illuminate were seeking new office space, a historic church would likely be at the top of the list!

In addition to the above, most are dog/pet friendly. I was even able to throw a tennis ball for one of the tenants' dogs. Sound familiar? Making A Point spokesdog, Lâffey the Pied Barbet, surely would be in heaven there. (Pun intended!)

So, the next time you are seeking office space for yourself or your organization, search for some great old church space. And if you have a dog, bring your pet with you and see if they declare the space suitable. Anything we can share with our pets is a blessing.

Chapter 33

Taking the Leap – Commercial Office Space vs. Home Office?

Anyone who knows me is familiar with an aspect of my "office story": my chance encounter with a university professor at a pet shop. While discussing her very rare breed of dog, we also touched on the topic of Illuminate's IWON (Illuminate Women Owners Network) program.

As we occupied space in the aisle of the store, the professor took my business card. She paused and said, "Wow, you have an actual office suite." It caught me by surprise. Of course, I have office space. But then I started considering many sole practitioners I know, and they all had one thing in common: they worked from home and never had an actual commercial office space. Would she have been so surprised if I were not a woman? Is it generally accepted that women work from home? Or was I taking her comment too far?

For me, the question often comes down to professionalism and, of course, money. Will potential clients think less professionally of you and your business if your company address is also your home? Will you need to meet in person with clients, and, if so, do you have a private club or community space to meet that can take the place of a traditional commercial office?

I do have a professional office space, and I also work from my home office sometimes. Some of the obstacles with the home office include being a pet owner.

One evening, during a Zoom session, all my animals were outside my home office door, trying to get in. They must have decided I had treats or something enticing behind the closed door. There was whining, scratching, barking, and meowing. They burst in near the end when the craftiest dog finally opened the door. All the dogs and cats rushed in. A "purrfect storm," as I called it!

I also live in an urban neighborhood with many historic 100+ year-old houses quite close to each other. Many of the homes have lovely yards and are frequently having work done. That means lots of contractors, landscapers, and delivery or service trucks. We also cannot forget the neighborhood dogs and the neighbor's in-ground swimming pool, where many swimmers seem to congregate.

There are many factors to consider when leasing commercial office space for your business. Retailers likely find it a necessity. Others, like professional business services, may view it as a "nice to have" but not a requirement.

Having your own commercial office space, regardless of size, may be the only path to a quiet and professional environment where you can have meaningful client conversations—free from the incessant "beep, beep, beep" of the neighbor's construction project or the cannonball splash in the neighbor's pool.

Shared common workspaces are another option. Most cities have some form of collective office sharing. It is certainly worth investigating for the affordability and amenities, such as access to higher quality equipment, like printers, that you may not want to invest in for your home office. While you may be looking for a quiet spot to hold a meeting, another rewarding aspect of this option is the social and networking opportunities; they are always marketing opportunities.

Dogs often outrun and outleap other dogs. It is the competitive world of lure coursing and dock diving. Much like our canine community, being mindful of the competition around you can work to your advantage.

Will commercial space help you take that leap and professionalize your firm's appearance? Or, perhaps, will you find yourself a home in a quiet part of town, save endless dollars, and utilize a UPS mailbox that has an actual street address, not just a PO box number, and no one else will be the wiser!

Chapter 34

Staring Down a Lease

Signing a lease for space for your business is both exciting and frightening. You will ask yourself: Is this the right place? Does it properly reflect my branding? Do I even like my potential landlord? And, most importantly, can I afford it?

When we went on the hunt for office space, we knew what we wanted and what we didn't want. There are so many acronyms that if you didn't have a background in real estate, you could easily become overwhelmed and, frankly, taken advantage of by the more unscrupulous landlords out there.

Here are some basic terms you will need to grasp when seeking the right location:

First is CAM, or common area maintenance. Many developers try to pass the full cost of the building they own onto their tenants. It is normally a percentage equivalent to the proportion of the building that your space occupies. For example, if you occupy 4,000 square feet out of a 40,000 square foot building, you will be responsible for paying 10% of the CAM each year. If you can, make sure the lease CAM excludes any maintenance on the roof, which can be one of the largest components of CAM. Otherwise, any profits you make could be owed to your landlord.

Besides CAM, you need to understand the three types of commercial leases:

1) Gross Lease – Under a gross lease, the tenant pays one fixed monthly fee. This fixed rent includes the base monthly rent, utilities, and services such as water, electricity, janitorial services, and building

operating expenses like property tax and insurance. This is the lease type that we have: one consistent amount every month, no surprises. It works quite well for a start-up or small business.

2) Modified Gross Lease – Where a commercial building allows for individual utility meters, one will more commonly find landlords offering Modified Gross Leases. The tenant pays for their utilities separately from the rent. This lease type has more variability than the gross lease but also allows the tenant to directly control the utility expenses. The rent amount will normally include property taxes and insurance, similar to a gross lease.

3) Triple Net Lease – This type of lease is most advantageous to the landlord and investor. Rent only includes rent. Utilities are extra, and there will be additional fees to cover maintenance, insurance, and taxes, the "triple" items of this type of lease. If the landlord/building's taxes or insurance increase significantly in any particular year, they can pass that along to the tenants. At times, landlords may call all of this either additional rent or CAM. Be sure to identify what is included in these items before you sign a triple net lease. My experience with this type of lease was essentially catastrophic. I learned the hard way; please don't follow suit!

You will have to look harder to find a gross lease, and it likely will not be in a downtown corridor Class A office building. However, taking out most of the variability in the other two categories of leases can be most beneficial to a small or burgeoning business. You can stare down these last two categories and make a less intimidating choice with a gross lease.

Remember to take control, get educated, and confront your lease; be its master. Don't let the size or reputation of your landlord intimidate you. Keep looking like we did, and you should be able to find a more financially feasible option for your start-up or existing small business.

Chapter 35

Ground-Up Construction

Expansion is exciting unless you are the one tasked with managing the project. Then, your relationship with the concept is much more complicated.

When embarking on a ground-up construction project, your top priority should be to choose an architect and a general contractor who have experience in your industry or a similar one. Do they understand the flow of your physical space? Can they provide references for past similar projects? And most importantly, if you are financing the project, have they successfully worked with your bank in the past?

This is important as your contractor needs to understand your bank's retainage and retention policies, whereby the bank withholds some of the funds. This can affect the budgeting process. If there are glitches or misunderstandings, you, as the project owner, may be expected to step in financially to bridge that dollar amount gap or negotiate a stalemate.

Another key consultant in any expansion is your attorney. They must have experience in commercial construction loans in the state where your expansion is taking place. Certain states, such as New York, have very specific requirements. Trying to use a cheaper or less experienced lawyer can be a recipe for disaster. To "build it once and build it right," make sure you have experienced consultants to help you.

When in doubt about any of your consultant's expertise, ask them how comfortable they are completing or reading the G702. If possible, request a redacted copy they recently completed or reviewed on a project. The AIA contractor form G702, Application & Certificate for Payment, is used to invoice a project if required. The form serves as both the contractor's request for payment and the architect's certification, which is mandatory from a bank's perspective and will determine whether or not your draw is paid. It is arguably the most important form in your construction financing process.

To ensure your project flows as smoothly as possible, try to avoid a property in flood zones, inexperienced contractors and attorneys, and spend some time researching G702s. The more you understand their financial details, the less chance the project will go off course.

Think of your project G702 as your dog's most beloved bone, and never lose sight of it. Guard a properly completed one as if the project depends on it because, from a bank's perspective, it does.

Chapter 36

Protecting Your Office Space

We live in a world with ongoing threats, such as crime, gun violence, mental health challenges, etc. That means it's always a good time to review your firm's security and protection protocols. Do you have the correct policies in place?

First and foremost, is your office space secure? "Secure" can be as simple as having your main door locked. Ideally, you would also have a deadbolt lock. For many small offices, this is the cheapest way to ensure that you, your employees, and any visitors are secure. Many office buildings also have steel doors installed, which can be far more difficult to breach than a wooden door. So, start with your office door or doors. Keep them always locked. Furnish your employees with "do not duplicate" keys. With these basic precautions, you are on your way to ensuring the first form of defense to keep your office safe and secure.

An additional safety feature for your office door is a peephole. This allows you to see the visitor before they enter your space. You can decide whether to open the door by looking to see who is there. If you choose not to open it, they will not be able to reach into your space without breaking the door down. Something as simple as a peephole can be the difference between a bad situation escalating and protecting yourself until first responders arrive. So, check your office door now, and if you do not have both a deadbolt and a peephole, the minimum investment to change out the door to include both safety features will likely be a good return on your investment. At the very least, you should be able to concentrate on your work and feel comfortable knowing that there are some precautions in place to protect you from unwanted visitors.

If your space is large or requires frequent public access, and a closed, locked door is not practical, make sure you have a security system. While more costly, it protects your office more comprehensively. Having a premises that includes a camera recording activity also helps if there is ever a situation that puts your firm at risk of liability. It can capture a slip-and-fall or a package that someone grabs. It is an extra layer of protection, safety, and risk containment. Most of the home security brands also have a commercial division, or you can install something as simple as Ring or Wyze cameras. Video footage of your space can be a true asset if it is ever required. It is difficult to dispute actions that have been captured on security footage.

The other option for ensuring safety in the workplace is to have a dog as part of your office. Dogs will often deter bad behavior, especially if it is a trained guard dog. Many breeds are good "alert" dogs—they will bark to alert you to visitors. You likely cannot rely on them to attack, but they will give you time to check your camera at the door or look through that peephole. A trained security dog requires early training and a trained handler who knows how to properly signal the dog for the next or correct reaction to a situation. Some buildings only allow service dogs, not pets, but if your office space does allow them, consider a good-sized dog as both a welcome addition to help reduce stress and the first point of alert in case of unwanted visitors.

Larger businesses often employ security guards. However, for most smaller businesses, such a security detail is beyond the owner's budget. It may be worth your peace of mind to consider leasing office space in a larger building where the landlord offers a security guard station where visitors must check-in. You almost always see this in Class A office spaces where these types of benefits are reflected in the rents.

Last but not least, ensure your policy manual includes security protocol. Advise employees on how to shelter in place, call 911, and ensure that anytime they come or go, the door, if possible, is always closed and locked. Workplace safety has become an important and critical factor in employee satisfaction in these modern times. Make sure your firm is protected as much as possible. Be alert. Being prepared for potential outside risks will contribute to a more relaxed and safe office culture.

Chapter 37

Mates in Their Crates

Speaking of dogs and your office space, many sole proprietors will look to share office space to reduce expenses and have collegial dialogue during long workdays. But can your office mate come in a crate?

We have all likely experienced walking into a business and having an animal suddenly appear to greet us. Usually, it's a dog, and most of the time, it is friendly. So, should Fido be allowed in all workspaces?

First, check your lease. Likely, there is a clause about pets on the premises. Most larger commercial spaces do not permit pets other than service dogs. If pets are allowed, there may be size or quantity limits.

Bringing a Great Dane or a toy poodle to the office is a very different experience. If your building permits pet dogs, should you bring them in?

Next, know your dog. If they don't like change or it takes them time to be comfortable with new people, they are likely not good candidates for office visits. If your dog is fearful of certain people, children, or loud noises, taking them to your office is, again, likely not a good thing for the dog or the people interacting with him.

We are aware of one larger commercial building that originally permitted dogs. That was until a dog bit someone, resulting in a lawsuit. The landlord's insurance carrier stated that they would not continue their insurance unless the building changed its policy. So, one "bad" pet owner eliminated the option of bringing in pets for all the other tenants.

If you have a well-behaved dog that will reduce stress in the workplace, make sure you set up a cozy crate for them. You can even brand the cover with your logo. A crate cover serves the dual purpose of providing a safe, quiet place for your dog while shielding any clients, visitors, or employees who are not "dog people."

After the example above occurred, and dogs were no longer permitted, while visiting a tenant on the floor at that commercial office space, I ran into a small Yorkie named Pierre Cardin. I wondered, surely if *that* Frenchman were allowed to visit, another Frenchman, namely my dog, the Marquis de Lafayette, would also be welcome. I checked with the landlord's office, and not only was the Marquis not welcome, but Pierre Cardin was asked to exit the building. Sorry, Pierre! But rules are rules.

So, before your office mate is one that needs a crate, consider all the consequences. It may be best to leave your pet at home, where they can watch the world from home base. However, if your dog has the right temperament and your space allows it, make sure you have a sign at the entrance and ensure there's a safe space to retreat to at any time.

Make it a point to remember their toys and treats. They are sources of exercise and stimulation, as well as great distractions. In addition, make sure you have food and water for him and that your schedule allows for walks to let them do their business. Barking, eating, and relieving themselves are behaviors you need to account for whenever your office mate comes with his own crate!

Chapter 38

Office Critter Control

We all take precautions at home to limit the impact of wildlife and nature on our personal living, but what about your office space? Have you critter-proofed it?

My corporate career was spent on the top floor of a downtown office building. The building had many owners over the decades I worked there. But regardless of who the owner was, we always had a "spider spectacle," as I liked to call it. Usually, in the heat of summer, spiders—lots of them, and very large ones—would make webs outside our windows. It was difficult to have a meeting, as we were all inevitably drawn to the spider spectacle occurring on the other side of the window. Our greatest concern was that they would make their way inside our offices.

One time, when I owned the dog swim center, I was out of town for my corporate job. I was at dinner with colleagues when I received a call to let me know a bat was dive-bombing the dogs in the pool. I calmly reminded the team that I was not even within driving distance. Did they call my business partner, who was in charge of operations? Did they call the landlord's 24-hour emergency maintenance number? Did they call our own maintenance engineer? Did they call our contractor? Sadly, the answer to all these questions was no. They called me, the president, sitting at a work dinner on the other side of the state.

Fast forward to my current consulting practice and the industrial office space that I share with my sister's architecture practice. As I was preparing lunch in the kitchenette, I noticed spots on the wall. Then I noticed them on the counters and the floors. Oh my goodness, they were bugs! Not just a few or a hundred, but literally thousands! They were covering our windowsills in the conference room and everything in the kitchenette. We called maintenance, who was right on top of it—baby mosquitoes. It took a few days of recaulking the windowsills and using natural bug spray, but they were finally gone.

So, what have I learned from all of these encounters with nature at an office? Be prepared. Stock natural bug spray, peppermint, or lemongrass oil. It smells good, and bugs hate it. If you have shades or drapes on your windows, consider closing them; these hide what you may not want to see. And bats, squirrels, mice, raccoons, groundhogs, and birds are curious creatures, always looking for a new place to call home or at least find food. Know your local laws on how to relocate them humanely and legally. And if all else fails, have your property management phone number close by; even better, in your phone contacts.

Leadership comes in many forms. If you encounter wildlife or nature at your commercial office space, call property management first. It is moments like those above where true leaders show themselves (or where you are reminded there is a reason you are the boss).

Section V: Points to Ponder

- Finding the right location for your business is critical to your brand. If you do not work from home, consider working with a real estate professional to identify the best place that expresses the identity of your business within your budget.
- Understand the different commercial leases available to you. Try your best to secure one that does not require you to provide a personal guarantee or pay the building's taxes (triple net lease). A gross lease, where you pay one total fee that does not change, is the ideal type for a small business that wants a set amount with no surprises.
- Secure your space, secure your equipment, provide security for you and your employees, and make sure your space is clean and free from all types of critters and bugs. You may be surprised by what springs up out of the field and into an office.

Section VI

Field Bank Run

Banking & Financial Services

Water retrieves can be performed by any dog, even if they do not particularly like water. These dogs will often circle the body of water and run along the banks or shores to determine how best to retrieve the target, given their lack of interest in swimming or getting wet in general. This is referred to as a bank run.

In the world of human business ownership, navigating an array of banking products can be quite similar. Many owners are not keen on having to understand and assess the variety of financial products available to them. While an owner can rely on their financial advisors, a good bookkeeper, an in-house office manager, or even their CFO (chief financial officer), it is beneficial to have a clear understanding of exactly which products and services can benefit your organization from a financial perspective.

- Chapter 39: Climb Above the Routine
- Chapter 40: Types of Business Payments
- Chapter 41: Check, Please!
- Chapter 42: The Importance of an Accurate Check
- Chapter 43: Bill Pay – How To Use It & Why
- Chapter 44: Clearing Time
- Chapter 45: To Swipe or Not To Swipe?
- Chapter 46: Working Capital

- Chapter 47: Leverage
- Chapter 48: Navigating Uncharted Waters – Export/Import
- Chapter 49: Researching Not-For-Profit Financials

Chapter 39

Climb Above the Routine

Like most businesses, you will have a primary operating checking account at a bank. But have you considered a second account? There are many reasons to do so.

First, consider that all vendors or consultants you use and pay by check have everything they need to attempt fraud on your account. Your check has your bank routing number and bank account number on it. In today's fraud-savvy world, that is all criminals need to try to hack your account. If you keep all your money in only one account and run all your transactions through it, the risk may be higher that your account may be hacked.

I have also seen clients use a second account solely to pay new vendors. Using it for that purpose allows you to become comfortable doing business with them. Once a pattern is established and you have developed a trusting relationship, you can revert to your primary account. This action again protects the bulk of your funds, as they would not have access to the primary operating bank account during your vendor/consultant onboarding process.

Another reason for multiple bank accounts for your company may be to isolate funds for various projects so there is no comingling. This is important if you are a prime consultant on a job; mixing specific job funds with your firm's operating account can be dangerous. Read your contract closely; the owner may require that a new account be opened just for the project funds. Even if your contract does not require a standalone checking account, it is good practice if specific funds are coming in for specific payments. It will be easier to audit and review and can provide you with peace of mind.

If you find yourself in the exciting position of embarking on the purchase of a building or the construction of a new building for your business, you should consider establishing a project account. If there is financing for the project, it is easier to track all the incoming sources and outgoing uses within a single account, one not mired in your everyday operational business transactions.

I have also seen companies establish a separate checking account for accepting deposits on credit card sales. If the bulk of your business is through credit cards, this could be tricky, as you want to make sure you have enough funds in your operating account at all times to pay overhead or unexpected expenses. Transferring money from the credit card acceptance account to the operating account could take more of your time, which could be better spent on the next project or sale.

There are automatic options for transferring money and moving it to additional deposit accounts. Research your bank's cash management options and discuss what is commonly referred to as a ZBA (zero balance account) structure. Fees that may apply for such an automatic sweep of funds may be worth your peace of mind. Evaluating these services is an important aspect of your relationship with your banker. Options are out there—make sure you are educated on them.

Finally, the most common reason for a secondary business checking account is to establish a payroll account. Firms will often transfer money for each pay period so that the funds are issued from a non-operating account. This allows your employees to remain one step away from having your primary account information. It's also easier for bookkeeping if you have a payroll service that is debiting the account and issuing the checks on your behalf. Once you begin adding employees to your business, evaluate this option.

Having multiple checking accounts can be beneficial for organizing your business's inflow and outflow of cash. Often, that second account can be free if you do not exceed certain volumes or transactions, or if you maintain a certain amount in all your accounts. Be sure to actively manage this aspect, and if your business is growing, it may be a good time to evaluate your need for multiple accounts and seek out a bank whose options and fees are to your satisfaction.

At times, we all need to take a step back or climb above our daily routines. Get a fresh perspective and ensure you are fueling the engine that is moving your business cash management practices forward.

Chapter 40

Types of Business Payments

If you are in business, you need to get paid. That is the simple part. The more complicated part is *how* you get paid.

Cash. Everyone loves cash. It is the international form of payment. It may be called different names in different countries, but it is still cash. You can touch it, feel it, fold it, clang it. And it is accepted just about anywhere for anything. If your business accepts cash as a form of payment, the most important aspect is storage and security. When there is a lot of cash in the office, even the most well-intentioned people can be tempted.

Unprotected cash poses a danger to a business in other ways, too. It requires a strict code of storage. Use a drop box bag from your bank to place it in. Once counted, go directly to the bank and deposit it. Most businesses handling a lot of cash make at least one daily visit to their bank. Use the ATM, the drive-through lane, or the night drop. (Often, the night drop bag is free, and it may require you to apply for a key from the bank to use it.) Most small business owners handle this themselves or assign it to the most trustworthy employees.

If your business is larger and/or takes in a lot of cash daily, there is an alternative offered at most banks. You can contract with a cash pickup service or have them install a cash vault or safe in your place of business. Cash vaults count the money as you deposit it, and that money becomes the property of your vault service. Your bank account is usually credited with that cash the same day or the next day. Depending on your contract, the service company makes daily or weekly visits to pick up the cash. This is a more expensive method of depositing your cash, but it is clearly convenient and usually one of the safest. However, again, you likely need to be bringing in thousands of dollars daily in smaller denominations to make this cost feasible.

The easiest method of payment is more likely accepting credit cards. There is no physical money passed, and you do not need to worry about making deposits at the bank or cash disappearing. However, it comes with a cost. The merchant credit card providers always charge a fee. Most are transaction-based but can be volume-based if you run a much bigger organization. Those fees can range up to around 5%. For a small business, that may be a high ask. Particularly for sole proprietors, it can mean the difference between a gain and a loss. Most retail businesses, regardless of size, need to accept credit cards from a purely competitive standpoint. There are independent processors and bank processors, so as always, do your research, ask for multiple quotes, and read the details. Most processors deposit your daily intake directly into your bank account within 24–48 hours.

"The check is in the mail." How often have you heard that one? Checks offer a lesser opportunity for disappearing on you but may take 3–5 days or longer to clear at your bank. Local checks from a local bank clear faster; those from across the country take longer, and banks vary in the time they take to clear checks. It really depends on your bank's clearing risk policy. So, make sure to ask your banker about clearing times. And, if you prefer checks, remind your clients often to make the checks payable to your business, NOT you as an individual. There is a reason you have an LLC or a corporation. Make sure your policy is clear on this.

Depositing checks is similar to depositing cash. Use an ATM, a drive-thru, a night drop, or sign up for your bank's scanning service. The latter may require a fee and may come with some technology requirements. Again, ask your banker; some banks offer the scanner free to very small businesses, but there usually is a monthly fee—just like using a credit card processing method. The benefits of depositing checks by scan from the office and avoiding physically going to the bank seem clear: less temptation for stealing by employees handling the checks and lower risk of other types of incidents. Usually, the availability of funds and clearing times are quicker.

And last but not least are electronic funds transfers (EFTs); EFTs are fast, and cash is never in hand. Wires, Automatic Clearing House (ACH), PayPal®, and Zelle® are the most commonly known EFTs. Not every bank participates with Zelle®, and it may not work with business accounts. Wires, ACH, and PayPal® may charge fees, which may be to both the sender and the receiver. Again, do your research and know the specifics of each method. Your banker should be able to review these options with you. One important element is that once a wire transfer has been sent, it basically cannot be undone. With ACH, it is possible, though not immediate; it usually takes 24–72 hours. There are benefits and costs to most of these options. The more you know, the better for you and your business.

When it comes to being paid for your products and services, what matters most is that you are paid. However, you have many options. Do the research with your banker and choose the method or methods that are most effective for your organization.

You work hard for your money and need to be rewarded for making informed choices.

Chapter 41

Check, Please!

I have encountered some rather surprising situations regarding payments.

Many small business professionals are comfortable with and accustomed to being paid by check. Not cash, not credit cards, not Bitcoin—just good old-fashioned checks. Some of the basic benefits? This form of payment carries little to no cost and provides an audit or paper trail for our accounting. It helps defray any incidence of fraud or embezzlement and makes it harder to simply forget to record the income, which can happen when you are responsible for everything.

So, why are people still trying to pay us in cash? They say, "Cash is king," but is it really? If you misplace it, you are out that payment. Period. If you are being paid in small denominations, those can blow away easily at an ATM. Of course, it cannot be scanned to be deposited. If we want to deposit it, rather than hold on to it for petty cash or other such expenditures, we are forced to go to a bank.

While ATMs are the quickest and most efficient way to deposit cash, there can be issues. Were you given a counterfeit bill, or is it maybe some wear and tear caused the machine not to read or accept it? It's hard to know without physically going inside a brick-and-mortar bank building. And this is exactly what happened to me once.

There are just too many scenarios where accepting cash in a non-retail setting can result in a high risk of losing that payment. And why should damaged or illegal bills become the business owner's issue? Retail shops usually accept cash and credit cards, and the fact is, they hardly accept checks—professional business services, such as consulting, are not retail, and you should not expect to pay in cash.

Chapter 42

The Importance of an Accurate Check

If you are in business, you will likely have at least one deposited check returned at some point. Returned checks are often associated with a lack of funds, but this is not always the case.

It is important to keep an eye on the details when either writing a check or depositing one. First, when writing out a check, focus on the payee—the business or individual to whom you are giving the check. It is imperative that you spell the name correctly. It sounds intuitive, but you may be surprised at how frequently the payee section is incorrect. This can cause the depositing bank to reject the check.

Second, is the date on the check correct? This can be a common mistake, particularly as the year turns into a new one. Most banks have a timeframe within which the check is considered "valid," usually around six months from the date issued. If someone gives you a check with the wrong year, and this is not discovered until the bank reviews its deposits, they will usually return the check for one with the correct date, foregoing any fees. The trouble starts if you have assumed the funds were available and written checks against them. You could be charged for that.

The next aspect to review before you deposit a check is the written amount, and by that, I mean the space where you write out the amount in words. I was once told by a banker that it did not matter what was written in the dollar amount or number section. The focus of electronic readers is on where the amount is written out in words. So, make sure it is legible, ensure it equals the dollar amount, and do not forget to include the cents. An illegible written amount can cause the check to be unreadable and returned. Many businesses use electronically prepared checks, which avoids this issue altogether, but many small businesses or individuals still write out their checks by hand.

And lastly, perhaps the single most important element to confirm when writing or receiving a check is that it is signed. An unsigned check will be returned.

We are aware of a situation where the client forgot to sign the check. The depositor did not notice that it was unsigned and deposited the check in a drive-thru lane. The bank employee also didn't notice. Two days later, the check was returned, and the bank contacted the depositor. Because the bank had initially cleared a small percentage of the check, the depositor had been able to pay a few expenses with those funds. To fix the chaos, the depositor had to retrieve the check from the bank, go to the client for a signature, and redeposit it back into the bank. The bank, recognizing its fault in allowing the check to be deposited by their employee, did not return the debit card amounts and did not charge an unavailable funds fee. Order was restored.

These are real-life examples that occurred to us or to companies we know. So, be aware of them for your business or when writing a check to a business. It takes only a few minutes to confirm the date, the payee, the written amount, and that the check is signed by an authorized signer on the account. So, "check, please" in this situation means you need to "check" for accuracy when issuing or being issued a paper check.

In the canine world, a dog will often "check in" with its handler/owner during any type of exercise or activity to ensure they are working correctly. Follow your dog's lead and take those extra few moments to ensure you have the correct elements on your check.

Chapter 43

Bill Pay – How To Use It & Why

While working with individuals or consumer clients, those who do not own a business, I saw a pattern. They struggled with *how* to pay my consulting firm with a good old-fashioned check. It was not about the funds but the function.

Why is this? I have identified that many individuals are deeply accustomed to paying for almost everything digitally now.

Businesses often pay vendors by check. Landlords, IT firms, health insurance premiums, trade association fees—the list is endless. For instance, I buy my health insurance through my chamber of commerce. If I use a credit card, I am charged a fee on top of the already high insurance premium. So, I write out checks quarterly. I enjoy using my business checks; they are a physical reminder that I created this entity and brand—all mine.

If you, as a business owner, want to accommodate those who are accustomed to paying online, you could research using the bill pay option at your client's bank or credit union. A client of mine started using this method to pay me. It was a little rough at first, but it is now humming along and seems to be a perfect payment method.

So, what exactly is bill pay?

As its name suggests, it is an online bill-paying option, often (but not always) offered at no cost by banks and credit unions. It allows the account holder to identify recurring or nonrecurring bills that should be paid directly out of their account, setting up details like the payment amount, date, recipient, and where it should be sent, etc. Most bill pay services send out a paper check, so keep that in mind when you are choosing the payment date. Note that the payment amount being debited from your account doesn't necessarily indicate that the check has been sent. According to bank rules, there can be a lag. The check may be sent too late if you don't account for that potential lag.

Talk to your banker to ensure that the timing will get the check to your payee and avoid my and my client's experience. In our case, the first check was about 10 days overdue. We learned the hard way. After the client adjusted the issue date with the bank, the checks always arrived on time, and we were both very happy. I don't have to discuss payments with them, and they don't have to worry about where their physical checkbook is. A win-win! I am grateful to the client who imagined a better way to pay me.

While this is the best way for an individual to pay a small business, usually one offering some type of professional services, bill pay may not work for a business paying another business. It might be more costly or better processed through business or commercial accounts.

Ask your accountant, your lawyer, your business consultant, and other trusted advisors if they can receive payments this way. If they do not accept credit cards, automatic bill pay is a great alternative for an individual to pay for small business services. As mentioned above, it is usually free to the personal sender. To our knowledge, most banks and credit unions, regardless of their size, offer this service.

Next time you find yourself wondering how best to make your payment to a small business, stop, assess your options, enjoy that you have options, and make a decision to try a new way to jump out of your dilemma. Likely, your service provider will appreciate the check sent to their business on time, the check made payable to the business, not to them personally, and the relief of being paid on time without having an uncomfortable collection conversation.

Try out the bill pay option on your bank account and know that you are making your transaction with a small business much easier for both them and yourself!

Chapter 44
Clearing Time

Small businesses, other than retail, are mostly paid by check or EFTs. Here are some ideas to help the check clear more quickly.

First, when possible, ask your client or customer if they can pay by ACH or wire. ACH stands for Automated Clearing House and is an electronic method of moving money among banks in the country. It usually takes up to three business days for the money to be in your account. It is a cheaper method than a wire, which is immediate and normally arrives in your account within hours. Chances are the client will decline, citing cost or administrative burden, or both. But it is worth the ask.

When electronic methods are not viable for your transaction, the traditional "check in the mail" will be the preferred mode of payment and receipt. Local, same-state checks will clear more quickly than those issued in states other than your own, which likely adds at least another day to clearing. If the checks are issued in another country, they must go through bank collections and can take up to three weeks, even if written in US dollars.

Assuming the majority of your checks are clearing through US banks, the key to expediting this clearing is your depository bank. Bank policy varies and some will often clear checks in one day, and that may include higher dollar checks as well. At a minimum, they will allow a percentage of the check to be available the next day.

Small businesses have higher risk profiles for overdrafts, and as such, certain banks may take three to five days or more to clear a check, even if it is local. Every bank's policy is different; some are negotiable. As a small business, make sure you inquire about check clearing times. If it is not to your satisfaction, tell them what you require. If they cannot accommodate you, consider a dialogue with another bank, until you find what works for you.

Banks are relationship-oriented. Often, the more business you have with them, the more they will value your relationship and the more incentives or rewards they can offer you. As a small business, they will normally wrap in or include your personal business. The largest banking product most true small business owners have is their personal mortgage. Therefore, it makes sense to start with the bank that holds the mortgage on your house. When they evaluate you as a potential business customer, they should have the ability to include that amount in the total amount and/or its profitability.

The longer and more extensive a relationship you have with the bank, the better off you will be in negotiating terms that suit you. Do not just settle for a weeklong clearing time. This is how you make a living—quicker clearing is a must. Speak with several banks before you choose which one is best for your business.

Set your own path for a clear journey among the daily obstacles. Understand your options and choose the quickest means to your destination. Clearing time for your check payments is one of your top priorities.

Chapter 45

To Swipe or Not To Swipe

How you collect revenue for your firm is an important decision. As we have mentioned, there are several methods available to you: paper checks, automatic EFTs (electronic funds transfers), cash (not recommended), and credit card payments. This last method can be the quickest, safest, and most secure way to accept client payments.

The old method of running a credit card through a machine to produce a carbon copy in person is long past. Now, you can swipe a card, some with a touchless option, or input a number on your cell phone with the appropriate link and device. Credit card processors have revolutionized how we transact with credit cards.

You may sometimes need to pay up to 5% per transaction in a card-not-present environment. So, why accept credit cards, given that there is a fee involved for their usage? Consider the benefits: cashless transactions (which reduce any opportunity for embezzlement, robbery, or just plain human error), immediate credit approval in lieu of potentially costly returned checks involving bank fees, and access to the money normally within 24–48 hours of settlement. How can you NOT accept cards when their use is just about mandatory in certain industries? Not doing so could be a competitive disadvantage in most retail environments.

Historically, professional service arenas have not widely adopted this payment method. This trend has reversed. Most attorneys, accountants, doctors' offices, and other professional service industries now accept payment via credit cards. Individual or business cash back or travel rewards cards add up to make a substantial impact on your bottom line. Many of your clients may prefer to pay by credit card as a result.

Your choices are quite varied. Always compare at least three providers and ask for the most competitive rate. Let them know you are shopping for the best value. More transactions and higher average purchase amounts will give you more buying power, so be sure to have those available to share with the credit card processing vendors. Your bank and third-party providers are just some of the options out there. An internet search will yield many lists ranking the top processors, so that is a great place to start.

Be sure to take the time to understand what you need—online versus POS terminals or a cell phone link. Know that Visa and MasterCard historically increase rates every spring, and that is a direct passthrough to you. Your bank or merchant provider likely cannot change that direct passthrough fee. So, negotiate on the amount above and beyond your Visa/MasterCard fee.

Ask your bank or merchant provider about enhanced fraud protection, such as tokenization and Address Verification Service (AVS). "Card present" transactions are almost always cheaper than "card not present" transactions due to the risk of fraud. Educate yourself with your merchant representative on all the available tools to collect and protect.

Bringing in revenue with credit cards may not be the solution for all businesses, but it is a viable alternative for many. The options and providers are extensive, so do your homework. Ask your banker for recommendations or inquire from a fellow business owner about whom they use and why. Check with any trade organizations or chambers of commerce to which you belong. Often, they have negotiated lower-rate programs for their members.

Remember, there is value in everything you do. Weigh the risk versus reward of adding credit card acceptance to your client's revenue collection options. As more and more individuals and businesses move away from the use of cash and paper checks, credit card processing can provide a more sustainable method of revenue collection in the long run.

Chapter 46

Working Capital

There is a saying in the banking industry: "The bank is willing to lend to you when you don't need the money." However, you can position yourself and your firm to be attractive to a bank's credit policy at any time.

First, what is working capital? From a strictly formulaic definition, it is your firm's current assets minus current liabilities. In essence, it is what you have left after you subtract what you owe from your assets, such as cash and accounts receivable. Often, particularly with Certified Business Entities working on government jobs, accounts receivable may approach 90+ days out. Many firms do not have the cash on hand to cover all the expenses during that three-month period. This is where bridging the gap between your cash on hand and the collection of your accounts receivable can be covered by a bank working capital line of credit. This facility will allow you to pay your bills or expenses on time while you wait for the receipt of your revenue from work already performed, that is, your accounts receivable.

Second, how to apply successfully for a bank line of credit is somewhat of a timing game. Your company will look most attractive to a bank when it is coming off a good or profitable year. Revenue must exceed expenses, plain and simple. Your equity in the firm should also exceed your liabilities owed. If you are a start-up or seeking a smaller line of credit, say $50k or less, many banks will just run the owner's credit score. If it meets their minimum threshold, there are unsecured lines of credit or lines of credit guaranteed to the bank through the US SBA (Small Business Administration). The criteria for these loans vary from bank to bank. Understand the terminology—you may have to personally guarantee the line of credit. Ask what the interest rate is based upon; usually, the prime rate is your easiest to track and understand. Ask if there is a 30-day out-of-debt period, where you are required to have the line of credit at a $0 balance, and be informed on whether the bank will be taking an all business assets filing on your business or if it will be unsecured, with no filing against your inventory, receivables, etc.

Lastly, and this is important, do not hesitate to approach banks. If you truly believe in your business, you will find someone to help finance your working capital needs.

Other than conventional financing, there are options with non-traditional financing sources. You will likely pay a higher interest rate on the money borrowed, but in the long run, it will likely be worth it as you expand your business. Ask your accountant or banker; they should know firms that will buy your receivables and, after a discount, provide you with immediate cash.

And while it is less preferable, many smaller firms have financed their working capital needs through a credit card, whether personal or business. Make sure to exhaust all financing alternatives before relying on a credit card. However, many credit card rewards programs, especially the cash-back options, can be advantageous if used properly and paid back monthly.

Working capital is an important element of understanding your business's cash flow and cash cycle. Take the time to meet with your financial advisors to discuss this topic. Know your options and act accordingly. Managing working capital is often the difference between just getting by or humming along. Plan for the future.

Chapter 47

Leverage

The Oxford Dictionary provides two definitions of the word leverage. One is what most people think of when they hear it: the exertion of force. The other is specifically for finance: the ratio of a company's loan capital (debt) to the value of its common stock (equity).

The basic premise of a company balance sheet can be defined by Assets = Liabilities + Owner's Equity. It is one of the first things anyone taking an introductory accounting course will hear and memorize. However, there is another formula that all business owners should be acquainted with. It does not require a degree, just an understanding of calculating a fraction and knowing the appropriate description to place in your numerator and denominator. It is surprising how basic mathematics from grammar school and high school can be used to determine a critical component of financial success in your business.

Even if your firm doesn't borrow money from a bank or capital source, knowing your firm's leverage should be included in your annual conversation with your accountant, your finance officer (if you have one), or your business partner(s) if you are not a sole proprietor. Why? Because it is a calculation that will drive any future conversations with your banker. It also helps you, as an owner, gauge the progress of your firm's success. Additionally, it may be the single calculation that makes or breaks your ability to grow with conventional borrowed funds. You never know when you may need to borrow funds from a lending source, and knowing your leverage and tracking your leverage can be an initial starting point for that discussion.

So, you may wonder, what is an ideal leverage ratio? As you might imagine, that can vary from bank to bank, depending on whether you choose an alternative lending source, and it can be influenced by many factors applicable only to your industry. As a basic guideline, a firm's total debt divided by total equity should be in the zero to 3x–5x range before conventional financing often seeks to utilize alternative lending. Alternatives may be in the form of government guarantee enhancements, such as an SBA guarantee.

Once your company has more borrowings than contributed equity, the term "levered" or "leveraged" is often used in banking and underwriting circles. The degree to which that leverage is acceptable for providing more lending is specific to your bank, whether you qualify for government enhancements like the SBA or an IDA (Industrial Development Agency) enhancement. IDAs may often have their own financing program, which will buy out or participate with a percentage of the bank's total lending package. Some banks will exclude secondary forms of government direct financing in their calculation; others will not. So, like anything in life, it pays to do your research and ask for more than one quote.

At your next annual meeting with your accountant, spend a few minutes understanding your firm's leverage ratio. It can be a defining ratio for your future growth plans or just a threshold you want to monitor as your business grows or changes.

A goal to have more invested in your company than borrowed should always be near the top of your list!

Chapter 48

Navigating Uncharted Waters – Export/Import

If you sell a product, any product, and your business continues to grow, at some point, you will find yourself in uncharted waters. This is when you draw upon your circle of trusted advisors and seek assistance on trade services.

Trade services is the term used by most commercial banks to describe bank instruments or products that assist business owners in moving products to places and/or with people previously unknown to them. It covers a wide area of trade, both domestically and internationally.

Many business owners will come across a Letter of Credit in their business lifecycle. This is an instrument that many landlords require from a new renter or with a long-term lease. An internet search for Letter of Credit provides this simple definition: "A letter of credit, also known as a credit letter, is a document from a bank or other financial institution guaranteeing that a specific payment will be made in a business transaction." This involves a bank underwriting analysis and often cash collateral. You may typically see this internationally when, say, a US company is renting space across the border in Canada. There are many types of Letters of Credit, so be sure to sit with your banker and perhaps their trade representative to understand how one may benefit your organization.

When conducting trade outside the country, there are many protective benefits to using Letters of Credit, Bankers' Acceptances, or other less common, customized tools. The goal of all of these is to ensure you are paid in a timely manner. A few instances when you will see these products offered to you include large new orders, international orders, and importing raw materials. Do not panic when you see these terms and find them unfamiliar. Your commercial banker should be there to guide you through these uncharted waters.

Business growth can be both exciting and a bit unnerving. Make sure you have a commercial banker as a trusted advisor, and take your time assessing the use of any of these trade services products. They come with great financial protection, but they are not cheap.

The nautical saying "steady as she goes" applies when venturing into the sea of uncharted trade services. But with proper training, guidance, and a good commercial banking coach, you will find your answers.

Chapter 49

Researching Not-For-Profit Financials

For small businesses or individuals who may wish to know more about the financial wherewithal of any not-for-profit organization, there is a public website to obtain that information. Most not-for-profits are required to file Form 990, and the best site that we have always used is one called GuideStar. It is free, and you can usually locate your organization by its name and state.

So, how useful can the information on this site be to you? Very, in my experience. It will tell you if the organization has been operating in a stable financial position. It will tell you the annual income and expenses for the organization. It will provide you with details on asset and investment levels. And you will be able to identify all the trustees or directors on its board.

A good team-building exercise is to identify a charitable organization where your team can volunteer together. Examples include food banks, homeless shelters, and low-income housing organizations. It is a good idea to research their financial stability to ensure you are partnering with a solid organization that has a track record of managing its mission well. As an owner or manager of a small business, encourage your staff to support these organizations after you have researched them and determined their fit and financial wherewithal for the future.

Who has to file the 990 form, you may ask? IRS.gov yields this answer: "An organization that normally has $50,000 or more in gross receipts and that is required to file an exempt organization information return must file either Form 990, Return of Organization Exempt from Income Tax, or Form 990-EZ, Short Form Return of Organization Exempt from Income Tax." Most organizations you will be looking to make donations to or partner with will likely fall into this definition. Therefore, you should be able to view their most recent 990 forms at GuideStar.org.

Do note that this applies to all not-for-profits, not just those with the tax-exempt 501(c)(3) designation. If you are considering joining a club of any kind, nearly all are organized as not-for-profit organizations.

I recently researched my old social club and the three other ones I was considering joining. Reviewing all of their 990 Forms online provided me with insight into their membership levels, their financial conditions, their cash balances, and their investment assets. I was also able to identify clubs with associated 501(c)(3) foundations, which normally act as a fundraising arm for capital campaigns around their real estate holdings. This research proved informative and allowed me to make the best decision.

Sniff out the best organizations for your pack. Do your research if you are considering tax-exempt donations, partnering with a charitable organization for company volunteering efforts, or just seeking informative insight into a club or organization that you or a family member are a part of or are considering for the future.

Section VI: Points to Ponder

- Understand your financials or work with an accountant in your circle of trust to guide you.
- Accepting credit cards comes with fees, sometimes as high as 5%, but you have guaranteed payment in your checking account, usually within a 48-hour period.
- Consider opening at least two checking accounts to separate payroll from sales or as an additional fraud precaution.
- Be sure to review the clearing time on your checks with your bank. Understanding the different options for expediting clearing time can help your cash flow.
- Knowing the many depository and financing options available to you with your bank cannot be overstated. Make that bank run and field all the support you can!

Section VII

To the Field & Beyond

Your Business as an Ongoing Concern

This section of this book covers everything from using email to maximizing efficiency to selling, closing, or retiring from your business. All great things will come to an end eventually, even this book, for now, at least.

Keep moving forward and consider all your options as your journey forges on, whether on the field or in the office!

- Chapter 50: Keeping It Confidential
- Chapter 51: Email Etiquette
- Chapter 52: Respecting the Response
- Chapter 53: Juggling Out-of-Office Time
- Chapter 54: Junk Email… or Is It?
- Chapter 55: The Golden Touch – Client Contact Strategies
- Chapter 56: Leveraging Free Social Media
- Chapter 57: Ready, Set, Expand, or Not
- Chapter 58: To Franchise or Not To Franchise
- Chapter 50: Managing and Mentoring to a Legacy
- Chapter 60: Live & Work Like Someone Left the Gate Open

Chapter 50

Keeping It Confidential

In the second year of our consulting business, our company successfully launched a new and unique women's exchange network, which I have mentioned previously in this book. It was called the Illuminate Women Owners Network (IWON). As we planned and started the group, we looked for an easily understood legal document to ensure confidentiality within the group. So, we conducted our research before consulting our attorney.

Initially, we considered our firm's standard non-disclosure agreement, intended for a circle of trust advisors when asked to work on a client's project. It became obvious that this document was not a fit for our women's group—because it goes into such depth, the term "overkill" was used while considering it. Some questioned whether we even needed any legal document at all.

I knew firsthand that personal and/or confidential information would be shared, even unknowingly. So, the answer is yes, and we needed it prior to the start of the inaugural session.

In the end, and on the advice of our legal counsel, we opted to use a brief document called Acknowledgment and Waiver of Confidentiality. It was less than two pages long, and despite having the requisite number of "Whereas" statements, each member understood it and agreed it was an appropriate document to sign, unaltered. Clients or groups should discuss it with their lawyers to see if it would work with their particular circumstances. It is surprisingly simple for non-legal professionals to understand.

Be like the dog world, where we train our animals to understand the command "quiet." Anything said confidentially or in private stays there. And know that your attorney will likely have the correct document to help remind you and enforce that confidentiality.

Chapter 51

Email Etiquette

We live in a world that frequently veers into the virtual. But does that mean we need to work at all hours?

It can be annoying to wake up on a Monday morning and find several emails from over the weekend. It's bad enough that the weekend is over, but since I enjoy routine, in these situations, I am torn between starting my day as I would like or responding to emails.

The first thing I do to avoid any conflicted feelings is not to look at my incoming emails on my phone until I am ready to engage with them. This puts me in control, not the email or its senders.

I also remind myself that if it were an emergency, the individual or firm sending the email would also text you and request that you check your email due to the urgency. Even most senders of emails alerting you to potential fraud, for example, from your bank or credit card companies, will also text you. So, make sure you set up text notifications for anything fraud related. Then you will know you are actually aware of truly urgent emails.

Third, and lastly, we would challenge you to consider when you send work-related emails. While it is becoming more common for people to include a disclaimer about the need to respond in their email signatures, for example, "My time to send may not be your time to respond. Please don't feel that you must respond right now," does it really make sense to send out that communication if it is a holiday or a Sunday evening? Perhaps writing it as a draft and sending it on the morning of the next business day is a better option, or using the Schedule Delivery Option to ensure it is sent during normal work hours. As mentioned, there is a growing awareness of both boundaries and the lack of them. So, consider everyone's mental health—your own included. Your clients, vendors, or employees will surely think better of you when you do not vex them with overnight emails.

We live in a constantly morphing, complicated world where personal time and work time can blend. With so many people working from home, make sure to take time for yourself, away from the work that defines you. Take control of your time, manage it well, and leave time for self-care, treats, and simple rest. Personal time is yours; don't lose it, either voluntarily or under perceived external pressure.

Chapter 52

Respecting the Response

It may seem daunting, but today's digital world requires each of us to be a master of our own domain and manage it appropriately with common courtesy. We have multiple modes of communication to choose from, and people—clients, vendors, suppliers, centers of influence—are contacting us in a variety of ways, including LinkedIn messaging, email, texts, phone calls, Facebook messaging, and Twitter. Are you keeping up? Are you responding in a respectful timeframe?

When possible, all messages should be returned within 24 hours of receipt. Depending on the urgency, or lack thereof, an immediate response is not always necessary, nor is it always viable. But a response *is* required, at least acknowledge receipt. Respect the effort to reach out to you. Ignoring it could be a poor business decision and defies common courtesy.

A lack of acknowledgment can also negatively impact your reputation. Reputation risk is real. Can you afford it? Most cannot.

Yes, many of us receive pesky solicitations. Some voicemails are not even in a language we can understand. You don't need to respond to those. However, choosing to not respond to a circle of trust member or an advocate, let alone a client or center of influence, can be received with hostility and lose you future business. Remember, if you can be anything, be respectful. Always use out-of-office reply options when you are on holiday or away for any length of time. It helps people understand that you are not ignoring them.

Remember the 24-hour rule; it could be the difference between respecting you or not, and choosing to do business with you or not. Try hard not to be the person who must be chased down for a response.

Chapter 53

Juggling Out-of-Office Time

Business owners universally seem to be short of one critical resource: time. Your out-of-office messaging can be helpful when used appropriately.

Most businesspeople utilize the "out of office" messaging when on holiday or at an all-day meeting or conference. This helps the recipient know that their message has been received but likely will not be addressed immediately. If you receive an out-of-office message, how do you react? That likely depends upon other information in the message.

A professional I knew utilized their out-of-office email message daily to inform anyone emailing them that day about what was happening. Rather than an "out of office" message, it was more like a constantly updated personal billboard. It was effective but perhaps overused. It made an impression, and as long as they kept it up to date (for example, "Hi, thanks for your email. I've stepped out to pick up my dog from daycare, back in a jiff!"), you would always know where the person was.

Utilizing out-of-office messaging can be a valuable tool to manage contact, but it needs to be precise and informative. Letting those who are trying to reach you know they won't be getting an immediate response is helpful. However, without accurate and timely information, it can frustrate your contacts more than anything else.

"Be bright, be brief, be gone" is a saying a colleague likes to use, and it applies to how you phrase your out-of-office messaging.

The three main elements it should contain are 1) how long you will be unavailable, 2) why you are unavailable, and 3) most importantly, offer an alternative if they have an urgent matter that needs attention.

Using your out-of-office message for communication is a smooth contact strategy and a simple gesture of courtesy. It should help further your interactions with clients, vendors, advisors, staff, and colleagues. Put it to work for you and use it to your advantage to help you balance your work game.

As I like to say, juggling too many balls is problematic for both dogs and business owners.

Chapter 54

Junk Email... or Is It?

While most "junk" emails are exactly that, if you don't monitor the junk folder, you may miss an important piece of correspondence. It has happened over and over at Illuminate. There is no rhyme or reason as to why certain emails, particularly those from known contacts, end up in the junk folder. Conversely, several that should be junk come through in my primary box, asking if I want to invest, offering to redesign my website, or applying for a loan.

I am particularly incensed by those true junk emails implying that my website could be better. That is clearly not the way into my office. My website is an extension of me and my brand; it was created by another women-owned business enterprise that is creative, responsive, and making it on her own. I love my website, and to insult it insults me.

After missing a few critical emails that somehow ended up directly in my junk folder, I adopted a policy to check it daily. Now, that could be a bit too frequent, but one missed important email is one too many.

For more reasonable monitoring, I would suggest doing it weekly and setting a recurring reminder. When you do check, look at both the subject of the emails and the names of the senders. If there is a sender that appears to be from a cell phone number, be sure to examine that email. It may be from a colleague who has inadvertently used their cell phone number email. This happened to me.

To reiterate, reviewing junk folders in your email is a critical element of your communications. Often, if an email is not responded to, the sender may choose to follow up with a call. But some may assume you chose not to respond, and that assumption could hurt your image. So, be proactive; set up a schedule to routinely review the emails in your junk folder. It could be the difference between "deal or no deal."

Chapter 55

The Golden Touch – Client Contact Strategies

With every customer, client, donor, and prospect comes the question we all have to answer: How much contact is appropriate? Too little may suggest we do not care enough, and too much may make us seem too persistent. It is a delicate balance.

As we have noted throughout this book, there are many ways to contact your clients, prospects, customers, or donors. First, there is the old-fashioned face-to-face method. Socializing is a powerful avenue for bonding with contacts and making them feel important. Visits, meals, and events are just a few options. However, the pandemic certainly made it harder to shake hands, give hugs, or high-five. In fact, many people now shy away from physical contact for fear of contagion.

While they can't entirely replace face-to-face contact, electronic means of communication, such as email, video chat, social media live video, social media messaging, or FaceTime, allow for a personal experience. It is effective and safe, and you don't need to worry about whether your attendees have been vaccinated.

We still have phone calls and conference calls that are not video based. And, of course, mail. We can send product or service recommendations through paper advertising or postcards. We can ask for donations via mail. We can apprise our customers, clients, prospects, patients, and donors of new options, new products, and new services. And we can send our thanks, congratulations, and condolences via cards through the mail. The handwritten gesture still makes a statement.

With so many options to contact others, it is important to research your prospects. Practice picking up cues from your existing clients and customers regarding how frequently they want to hear from you and through what methods. Donors may expect a higher level of touch and a more expensive or personalized experience. Lunches, dinners, golf games, and sporting or music venues in a box—these are all acceptable and sometimes expected forms of gratitude with higher-end clients or donors.

The dog world uses the touch command to gain the focus and attention of a dog, particularly when recall is important. This is not all that different from people trying to gain the attention of other people, where a sale, a reward, or a treat is the ultimate outcome. Again, our worlds collide.

Chapter 56

Leveraging Free Social Media

Focusing on social media to keep your business "fresh" with your target clients is an excellent use of any spare time you may have. If you do not have a social media presence, you need one. Many of the platforms are free.

Before I left my corporate position, a colleague asked me if I would be placing a full-page ad on the back cover of our local business paper to plaster my face and new business out there. I laughed.

First of all, the cost would not warrant the return for my niche business. Second, I planned to embrace free advertising on various digital social media platforms. To prove that this is effective, I can attest that my first paying client, along with another acquired client, came from social media: they were Facebook friends of mine. One was not even local.

LinkedIn, Bluesky, Facebook, Instagram, and blogs are all platforms that Illuminate has embraced during its lifecycle to market and advertise our brand. While we have the budget, we have chosen not to use any of the platform levels that require users to pay. Building a brand takes time, resources, and a definitive plan on where you wish your brand to go. The path is not always clear from day one, and it will likely shift many times during the life of a business. Social media allows that journey to help shape the future of a business. It may take your business on a path not yet considered or planned by the owner, and without cost, which is a great advantage over traditional business advertising strategies of years ago.

LinkedIn is a good platform to reach corporate executives or clients; you first need to set up your business profile. The basic platform, which I have used since it was developed, has been a useful channel to share my articles with centers of influence from my previous career. It is an effective and efficient way to reach executives and professionals and garner their interest in your product or service. Additionally, it is a helpful source to identify and target clients to tout your brand. It can provide the pulse of the economy at your fingertips and allow you to search for local or distant new markets. If there is someone you wish to reach out to, you can see if any of your contacts are "linked in" with them. Ask those contacts to make an introduction. That is a very productive manner for prospecting. Your contacts usually will not decline such a request; it is, after all, why everyone is on this platform. Make the most of it!

Bluesky, Instagram, and Facebook each allow your business to reach a vast individual marketplace. Use your hashtags appropriately, tag locations or institutions in relevant posts, and watch how retweeting or reposting can help your products or services reach untapped channels. Instagram is a terrific platform to visually showcase what your business has been up to or is about to embark upon and can be linked to Facebook so the same post occurs from just one platform. We are a visual species; use it to your advantage. Pictures are eye-catching compared to just words. The more your brand is seen, the greater the chances it has to succeed.

Blogs are the most intriguing form of free business advertising. They cannot be streams of consciousness essays. Choose an appropriate name for your blog, adhere to common themes, and choose a consistent timeframe (e.g., Making A Point is posted every Monday). The content should inform your readers about the varied topics that either are your business or impact your business. Make it interesting, use relevant, enjoyable photos, and make it worth their time. Seek feedback from your audience. Do you have a subscribe button on your website? That makes it easy for readers to effortlessly receive your blogs. Ask them to share your content and remember the other social media platforms. Share your blog on every one of them!

And a tip: once you copy the link and it has been auto formatted by the platform, delete the actual linking URL that shows up on your post. Those are often annoying and lengthy. We have found you can erase that eyesore and just have the blog itself show up with the associated image. Bring your reader's eye right to the photo and the content; they do not need to be distracted by anything else.

It is always an ideal time to learn about the free aspects of social media and educate yourself on its best use relative to marketing your business, your brand, and your effort. While you are at it, make sure you share and repost others' content. It is the singular form of corporate flattery you can bestow on a fellow business, and hopefully, they will return the favor. Your audience and, perhaps, your next client are just a post or share away!

We are all in this together. Make that sentiment work for you by engaging with social media and telling your story and others' when appropriate. It's working for us; we hope it can work for you too.

Chapter 57

Ready, Set, Expand or Not

When is the best time to expand your business? Or the better question may be, when do you know it is the right time to expand?

When you begin to look beyond your service area or your product lines, you are likely ready to expand. Embrace it. Seek input from your circle of trusted advisors. Detail what you will need to accomplish this—both human and financial resources. Turn this into an exciting time for you and your company.

We met with a woman business owner who explained how her path to expansion seemed to find her. The right time to hire an assistant, a chance connection with a complementary service provider, a gala seated with similar entrepreneurs. The universe was trying to talk to her, and she decided to listen.

Expand for the right reasons. A new market or industry is in need of your product, a new group of clients is interested in your services, and a happy client opens up a new community to you and your services. These are all great examples of why and when to expand.

Competition is a natural drive for most of us, especially for those who have already founded a business. But don't let that be the only thing driving your decision to expand. Identify the positive attributes, lean on your advisors, seek client input, and move forward when you are inspired, excited, and ready to make it happen. You will know when all the stars align and the sensation of accomplishment is already on the horizon.

When it comes to expansion, timing is everything. Seek the guidance, do the research, and identify the resources. Your pathway may soon be "Illuminated." If you do this at the right time with the right resources, your firm's future will be bright. Don't forget your sunglasses!

Chapter 58

To Franchise or Not To Franchise

If your small business has a unique product or service, or if the demand outpaces your anticipated supply, you may find yourself wondering about franchising. Is it a path of exploration for your business?

When I co-owned an indoor dog swim center, during the first quarter of operation, we asked ourselves this very question, as our business was unique. In fact, so unique that we had a dog business in town send "spies" to covertly investigate our eco-friendly filtration. In retrospect, what a compliment. At the same time, an out-of-town water dog club with locations on the East Coast contacted us about franchising. The rest of this section is a synopsis of our experience.

First, we were honored. Second, we were overwhelmed, and third, we did not pursue it. I had a working banker's knowledge of franchising. I reached out to the CPA firm in town that I knew had extensive experience with franchising, both on the franchisor and the franchisee sides. I quickly learned some of the basic tenets of franchising and that our fledgling business did not meet the criteria.

You need to be making, not losing, money as a business if you want to consider franchising. That's hard to do when you are just a startup that requires a hefty equipment investment. So, right away, I knew we did not qualify.

Time is the second requirement. Neither my business partner nor I had much, as this was a side business to our full-time professional careers. You must be willing and able to devote significant time to train the franchisee about your operation. That entails providing them with essentially a "how to" manual, from concept to profit-making.

Supporting them with branding, marketing, advertising, operations, etc., all falls on you as the franchisor. Think of it as a "turnkey" effort. This means all the franchisee has to do is turn the key to open the door, and they can start operating, per your instructions, and make a profit. Again, this is something we could not provide.

We did offer the water dog clubs the option to buy our naming rights, use our logo, etc., but they were not interested. They did not want the risk of having to operate on their own. While we didn't participate in this opportunity, we all learned some very valuable information.

If you meet the first two criteria I mentioned—making a profit and having time to do everything related to formulating the franchise—your next stop should be an experienced CPA and attorney. Franchise bankers exist and are normally included in the commercial/corporate bank; engaging their expertise means your company must meet several size thresholds, which a small business usually cannot. Often, this niche group will only work with the largest franchises in the country or the globe.

On the franchisee side, the SBA (Small Business Administration) may be a good place to inquire about which of their programs can be used to buy into a franchise. New franchisors must understand which banks have the appetite for franchisee lending. It may help you sell your concept to prospective buyers if you can direct them to a bank that is experienced in providing SBA-backed loans for start-up franchisees. While this is not a requirement, it is always good to be able to show you have done your research.

When it comes to expanding your product, service, or geographic reach, there are options. Certainly, one of them is to consider if franchising is the right choice for you. Do your research, meet with your circle of trusted advisors, and find an experienced CPA firm and attorney. It will protect your business and any potential interested parties in the long run.

Do your research and evaluate your next move before you pounce on an opportunity.

Chapter 59

Managing and Mentoring to a Legacy

There are events in your life that change its entire trajectory. And there are times when you are reminded that the most important aspect of one's job may not be the revenue you raise but the lives you impact along the way.

If you are in a leadership role at your firm, you have a unique opportunity to distribute the wealth of information you have acquired along your professional journey. As that leader, it is incumbent upon you to foster those around you and create the next generation of leaders. If you were lucky enough to have a mentor help you on your journey, you likely understand the need to pay this forward. And if you were not lucky enough to have a guide along your path to success, imagine how you can change someone else's path.

I had the opportunity to reconnect with an ex-colleague. She reminded me that my greatest impact from my previous career was not in seeking the top position for new business achieved. It was not the success I assisted clients with. Rather, it was the legacy of mentoring, not just her, but a few others along my travels.

I was privileged to be involved in hiring a few special colleagues early on in my career. I was always humbled when each made the same comment: "Joanne taught me what I needed to succeed here." They were young, eager, and had the intelligence to surpass any success I may have achieved. I will always take with me that I played a small part in their upward trajectory. I worked hard to ensure that they had support and guidance on their path, as my mentor had done for me at the beginning of my journey.

If you are in management and/or leadership, take stock of those around you. Take ownership in providing them with the tools to succeed and move upward. Trust them to make decisions without you, even if they stumble along the way. You can't do it all and shouldn't do it all. Do not hold up progress by being an obstacle—be the leader who looks ahead. It is the best way to help your business flourish, especially beyond your time there.

Chapter 60

Live & Work Like Someone Left the Gate Open

In the world of dog sports, dogs are trained to sprint using a tool called Fast Coursing Ability Test (Fast CAT®); it's a timed 100-yard dash. For small business owners, we can also work like someone left the gate open. While I have written about many of the challenges solopreneurs and small business owners face, there are also many rewards to choosing this professional path.

Making your own schedule is one of the top benefits of being your own boss. You are not beholden to a preordained workday. Make your schedule reflect the times when you are most productive. You are in charge—no one else, and no corporate mandate or policy manual. Engage to be efficient, not just to be present. That approach often does not have set time frames. Make the most of your flexibility.

If someone asks you to attend a meeting, virtual or otherwise, at a time that doesn't work for you, such as 6:30 a.m. or 7:30 p.m., you likely have the option to just say no. Own your time; do not be taken advantage of. Unless it is your largest client or a new prospect you are aiming to impress, as the owner of your business, you have earned the right to set your own expectations with colleagues and clients.

One of the most liberating features I have discovered on my own is the ability to dress casually. The stuffy suit, the high heels, the uncomfortable blazer—all gone. In their place, I choose jeans, comfortable clogs or boots, colorful sweaters, and casual shirts. It is surprising how inspiring comfort can be!

The last element of being your own boss that I embrace every day is choice. The choice to take on a client or pass, the choice to decide you need to take a personal day, the choice to work from home, your backyard, or just not to work at all that day. Of course, choice may be impacted by deadlines or client expectations, but in the end, you are the boss, and it is your choice.

Make sure you reap the benefits of owning your own business. Take the time, as your schedule permits, and enjoy your decision. And live, or in this case, work, like someone left the gate open!

Section VII: Points to Ponder

- Manage your out-of-office, junk email, and response time to emails. This flow will set you up for better operational management.
- Commit to yourself to be disciplined in your business.
- Leverage social media. Much of it is free and can maintain that operational flow to maximize efficiency and opportunity.
- Enjoy what you do; your business is an extension of you.
- Most importantly, live and work as if you left the gate open!

About the Author

Joanne Campagna is a retired commercial banking executive, was a co-owner of an indoor dog swim center, and is now a solopreneur leading Illuminate Business Consulting, LLC, where she has written "Making A Point" weekly blogs since founding her company in 2019.

Her great passion in life is the Barbet, or French water dog, breed. The breed's joie de vivre for all things fetching-related, including pointing at squirrels, flushing birds, and retrieving balls or toys thrown to them, inspired her to write the weekly small business blogs with a sporting dog twist and, eventually, compile them into this book.

Joanne holds both a bachelor's degree and an MBA from the University of Buffalo, is a graduate of the American Bankers Association Commercial Credit Training Program, the FBI Citizens Academy, Leadership Buffalo, and was a Business First Women of Influence Winner in 2016. She also chaired the CanAm Council for a few years at her local chamber of commerce.

Joanne participated in the Executive Exchange Program at The Buffalo Niagara Partnership for several years, which provided her with direct experience in business leadership programs, inspiring her to create IWON (Illuminate Women Owners Network), an idea exchange network for professional women leaders. It is not surprising that her inaugural group was built from friends she knew through her pet/animal activities.

Joanne is a global traveler, enjoys reading, both fiction and nonfiction, engaging with her Barbet, and is a passionate small business advocate. Blending both her love of dogs with her knowledge and expertise in small businesses in this business commentary is a dream come true.

Thank you for reading our journey and "Making A Point". Supporting small businesses is essential to the growth of our economy and our lives.

Please follow us at Making A Point on www.illuminatebc.com, Instagram, Facebook, Bluesky, & LinkedIn.

Acknowledgments

I would like to acknowledge the contributions of many people and dogs who made this book possible.

First, a sincere thank you to my book agent, Jane Creech, of Rooster Books, Inc. Her expertise, patience, and kindness saw me through this entire process.

Second, I would like to thank my sister and office suite mate, Barbara Campagna. Without her many experiences as a sole practitioner, several of these chapters would have never been written.

Additional thanks to Lisa Samar and Nicholas Switalski, who helped achieve my design goals. Your vision and creativity were instrumental to the beautiful cover.

Thank you to my village of peer reviewers and those who provided encouragement along the way, including Elizabeth Howard, Acea Mosey, Kelly Hayes McAlonie, and the many readers who sent words of thanks and praise for the thoughtful topics.

And, lastly, to all the dogs, past and present, in my life who inspired the title with their focus and antics—Finley, Kolby, Lafayette, Trevi, and Zune—you truly have made a point in my life!

www.ingramcontent.com/pod-product-compliance
Lightning Source LLC
LaVergne TN
LVHW091531200926
848483LV00002B/366

* 9 7 9 8 8 9 2 2 2 5 6 3 2 *